"The energy infusing their words tells you the authors enjoyed every booted step . . . ."

–Southern Living

"An excellent . . . guide."

–Sport and Fitness Journal

"Russ Manning and Sondra Jamieson have moved the Big South Fork National River and Recreation Area into the close-and-accessible category."

–The Knoxville News-Sentinel

Books of Note: "A pocket-sized hiker's guide to one of the newest national parks."

–Backpacker

"Russ Manning along with Sondra Jamieson . . . has written an excellent guide book on the Big South Fork."

–The Roane County News

". . . describes hikes in an easy-to-follow manner"

–The Oak Ridger

"Campers and hikers have been quickly snatching up this . . . little paperback."

–The Knoxville Journal

". . . a great beginner's guide to a still relatively uncrowded wilderness."

–The Memphis Commercial Appeal

". . . hold(s) the key to indescribable treasures of Tennessee up on the Cumberland Plateau."

–Tennessee Librarian

for Liane Russell,
Tennessee Citizens for Wilderness Planning,
and the Big South Fork Coalition

for their leadership in preserving
the Big South Fork

TRAILS OF THE BIG SOUTH FORK

NATIONAL RIVER AND RECREATION AREA

A Guide for Hikers, Bikers, and Horse Riders

A Tag-Along Book
by Russ Manning and
Sondra Jamieson

Third Edition

Mountain Laurel Place
Norris, Tenn.

Mountain Laurel Place assumes no responsibility or liability for accidents or injuries suffered by persons using this book to explore the Big South Fork National River and Recreation Area.

Third Edition; copyright © 1995 by Russ Manning and Sondra Jamieson. Second edition, *The Best of the Big South Fork*, copyright 1990. First edition, copyright 1989.

Printed on recycled paper.

Printed in the United States of America.

ISBN 0-9625122-5-7

Front Cover: Angel Falls
Back Cover: Yahoo Falls

Published by

    Mountain Laurel Place
    P.O. Box 3001
    Norris, TN 37828
    (423/494-8121)

Contents

Leatherwood Ford and East Rim (Map 4)   44

West Entrance (Map 5)   70

Middle Creek (Map 6)   90

Blue Heron/Bear Creek/Yamacraw Bridge

Yahoo Falls (Map 13)

Pickett State Park and Forest (Map 14)

Acknowledgments

We are grateful to the National Park Service staff at the Big South Fork National River and Recreation Area, led by Superintendent Lee Davis, for their support in the preparation of this book. Park Ranger Interpreter Howard Ray Duncan, NPS Archeologist Tom Des Jean, and Chief of Interpretation Steven Seven provided valuable information about the park and the history of the region. We appreciate the support of Park Ranger Management Assistant Ron Wilson.

Chief of Maintenance Fred Kelley, Trail Crew Leader Wally Linder, Roads and Trails Supervisor Palace Anderson, and Forestry Technician Jeanne Richardson provided trail information. We appreciate Richardson sharing with us map information and proposed revisions to the Roads and Trails Management Plan.

We also thank Jeanne Richardson, Howard Ray Duncan, Wally Linder, Ron Wilson, and Fred Kelley for reviewing all or part of our draft manuscript.

We thank Pickett State Rustic Park Manager Billy G. Smith for reviewing the section on Pickett State Park and Forest.

The Big South Fork

River and Gorge

On the Cumberland Plateau in Tennessee, the Big South Fork of the Cumberland River flows north into Kentucky, draining some of the most primitive and isolated lands in the eastern United States.

Before there was a national river and recreation area, local people who loved the outdoors spent many seasons wandering the forests and exploring the gorges of the watershed. In those days, the Big South Fork was Tennessee's and Kentucky's best kept secret.

Our first encounter was along the road from Oneida that crossed the river at Leatherwood Ford, now TN297. Then, it was a gravel road that precariously dipped into the gorge and crossed the old wooden bridge that still spans the river. From Leatherwood Ford, we explored along the river one afternoon looking for Angel Falls. We expected a waterfall, but found instead a huge rapids where the water rushed down river.

Later, we hiked to Twin Arches at a time when most people thought the idea of such a phenomenal geologic structure in Tennessee was preposterous, but it wasn't a tall tale, just hard to find. In the Kentucky portion of the watershed, we wandered through the site of the abandoned Blue Heron Mining Community; only the old rusting tipple, used to separate the coal, remained.

The threat of eventual development of this isolated area convinced many that the Big South Fork needed protection before its wilderness character was lost forever. This brought about the establishment of the Big South Fork National River and Recreation Area. Now tagged with a federal initialism, BSFNRRA, the Big South Fork is still a land of isolated river gorge, natural stone arches, numerous rock shelters, slender waterfalls, and old homesites linked by 300 miles of trails and many more miles of old roads. In this guide, we describe these routes for hiking, horseback riding, and mountain biking in the Big South Fork and surrounding area.

Norris, Tenn.

Russ Manning and
Sondra Jamieson

Park History

Federal involvement with the Big South Fork dates from 1881, when the Army Corps of Engineers conducted a study for improving navigation on the river. No action was taken.

Then in 1933, the Corps proposed a dam at Devils Jump, a rapids in a narrow part of the river gorge in Kentucky. The dam was originally projected to cost $200 million and would have been the highest dam in the East. Although proposed for Kentucky, the dam would have flooded the river gorge in Tennessee.

During the 1950s and '60s, the Devils Jump Dam was authorized several times in the U. S. Senate but never passed the U.S. House of Representatives. Over the years, other studies recommended flood control lakes, dams at other sites, and pump storage facilities.

In 1966, a local conservation group, Tennessee Citizens for Wilderness Planning (TCWP), set out to find some kind of permanent protection for the Big South Fork and to put to rest the dam and lake proposals that kept being resurrected. TCWP first tried to get the Big South Fork included in the Tennessee Scenic Rivers Bill that was soon to pass the State Legislature. But when the bill passed in 1968, the BSF was excluded from the list of rivers.

Then TCWP turned its attention to an impending national bill. An early study by the now-defunct Bureau of Outdoor Recreation had designated the Big South Fork as worthy of being included in a National Wild and Scenic Rivers Bill. But when the national bill was passed, also in 1968, the Big South Fork was again excluded.

Because of the public interest generated by TCWP, Congress then requested new studies on the Big South Fork. One was to examine new dam proposals and a second was to study alternatives. The Corps of Engineers, the Bureau of Outdoor Recreation, the U.S. Forest Service, and the National Park Service were to be involved in the studies.

TCWP acted as an advisory group for the alternatives study, which when made public presented several suggestions for what to do with the Big South Fork, including national recreation area, national forest, national park, and scenic river. With the public sentiment apparently behind saving the river, the decision was made not to bother publishing a dam study.

During this time, TCWP gained strength by forming a union of various conservation groups, the Big South Fork Coalition. The group was headed by Liane Russell, a research geneticist living in Oak Ridge who along with her husband, Bill Russell, also a research geneticist, helped found TCWP.

The Coalition worked with then-Senator Howard Baker, Jr. to draft a bill calling for a combination of national river and recreation area. Introduced in 1972 as part of a water resources bill, the legislation would have automatically given the Army Corps of Engineers authority over the proposed new area. The bill was pocket-vetoed by President Richard Nixon for reasons having nothing to do with the Big South Fork.

The BSF Coalition took advantage of this delay by rewriting the bill so that management of the area would be turned over to the National Park Service after establishment by the Corps of Engineers. The Coalition thought the NPS would bring more experience in preservation and conservation to the task of managing the proposed new national river and recreation area.

The legislation was reintroduced as part of the 1974 Water Resources Development Act. Passed and then signed into law on March 7, this act authorized the Big South Fork National River and Recreation Area, encompassing 123,000 acres.

In the intervening years, the Army Corps of Engineers purchased lands, laid out trails, and built visitor facilities as funding became available. The National Park Service took over management on an interim basis as pieces were completed. At this writing, some lands have yet to be purchased.

In November 1990, the U.S. Congress passed legislation authorizing the official transfer of the park to the National Park Service. The transfer from the Corps of Engineers to the NPS was officially recognized on August 25, 1991, at the dedication of the new park headquarters. The ceremony was also a symbolic dedication of the Big South Fork National River and Recreation Area (BSFNRRA).

3

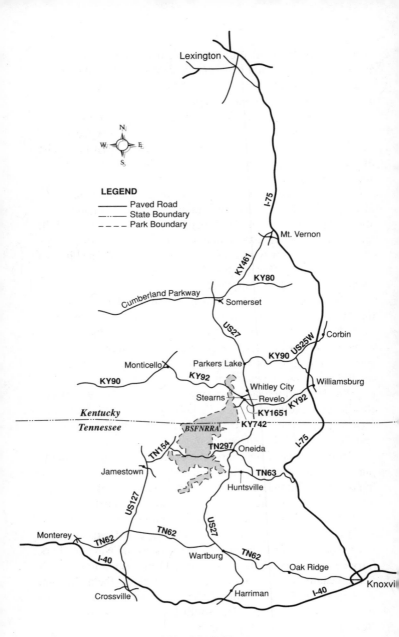

Map 1. Getting to the Big South Fork

4

Getting There

The Big South Fork National River and Recreation Area lies atop the Cumberland Plateau west of I-75 between Lexington, Kentucky, to the north and Knoxville, Tennessee, to the south.

From the north on I-75, you can approach the Kentucky portion of the BSFNRRA by exiting at Mt. Vernon and taking KY461 and then KY80 southwest to Somerset where you'll turn south on US27. You'll eventually reach a west turn on KY92 toward the community of Stearns. A new visitor contact station lies off to your right soon after the turn. In Stearns, take KY1651 south to Revelo and turn right on KY742, which becomes Mine 18 Road, to get to the Blue Heron Mining Community. You can also reach the park from the north on I-75 by exiting onto US25W near Corbin and heading southwest to a turn west on KY90 to US27 and then turning south toward Stearns.

Traveling from the west in Kentucky, you can go east on the Cumberland Parkway to Somerset and then south on US27 toward Stearns. Or you can take KY90 east and then, in Monticello, pick up KY92, which eventually crosses the Yamacraw Bridge over the Big South Fork and leads into Stearns.

To approach the Tennessee portion of the park from the north or the south, take TN63 west from the I-75 exit for Huntsville and Oneida. You'll pass through Huntsville and reach US27; then turn north to Oneida where you'll pick up TN297, which enters the park, crosses the Big South Fork River at Leatherwood Ford, and takes you by the Visitor Center at Bandy Creek on the west side of the river.

If you are traveling from the west in Tennessee on I-40, get off at the Monterey exit where you'll pick up TN62 and continue east to a junction with US127. Turn north to Jamestown; continue north and turn northeast on TN154. You'll come to TN297 where you'll turn east to reach the Bandy Creek Visitor Center. Farther east on I-40, you can pick up US127 headed north at the Crossville exit, and even more to the east, you can reach Oneida and the east side of the park by taking US27 north from the Harriman exit. If you're in the Oak Ridge area, take TN62 northwest to Wartburg, where you'll pick up US27 headed north.

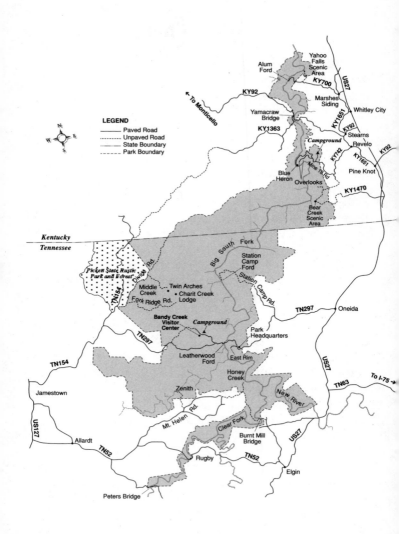

Map 2. Access within the Big South Fork

6

Geology

At one time, ocean covered portions of what are now Tennessee and Kentucky. Great deltas formed where rivers flowing from Appalachian highlands to the east met this sea along a shoreline in the area that would become the Cumberland Plateau.

About 300 million years ago, a final episode of Appalachian mountain building began. The new mountains that formed in the east eroded quickly, depositing a layer of sand and gravel more than a hundred feet thick over the entire delta system of what was to be the plateau region. Later, the shoreline settled and the sea reinvaded, dropping its silt. This cycle of mountain building to the east, followed by erosion and deposition of sediment, repeated in several pulses over millions of years during a time geologists call the "Pennsylvanian Period."

Under the increasing weight, these piled-up layers consolidated into rock. The thick sand and gravel layer first laid down became an erosion-resistant Pennsylvanian sandstone.

Later, the land rose high above sea level in three intervals of secondary uplift as less dense rock below was forced upward by surrounding dense rock. Erosion immediately began lowering these new mountains but slowed when the resistant Pennsylvanian sandstone was encountered. So after millions of years of erosion a plateau still stands 2000 feet above sea level. Called the "Cumberland Plateau" in Tennessee and Kentucky, it is part of the Appalachian Plateaus Province that stretches from the southern border of New York to central Alabama.

As the Clear Fork and New Rivers converge to create the Big South Fork, which then flows north across the Cumberland Plateau, the river system carves a deep gorge, exposing the resistant sandstone layers in the bare rock walls that line the rim. Side streams flow over breaks in the sandstone to form waterfalls. In exposed hillsides and ridges, erosion sweeps away soft layers under the hard sandstone, creating numerous rock shelters and natural stone arches.

These geologic features make the Big South Fork one of the most interesting areas for outdoor recreation in the eastern U.S.

Human History

The upper Cumberland Plateau area that encompasses the Big South Fork was originally occupied by a succession of native American peoples, from the Paleo-Indians, through the Archaic and Woodland cultures, to the Mississippian tradition.

These early inhabitants were originally big game hunters. By 1000 BC, they had developed pottery and led a more refined existence, catching fish in the rivers and streams and gathering nuts and berries. Around 900 AD, they began to grow some of their food and, by 1000 AD, were experienced farmers, growing primarily corn and squash. This led the people to move to the broad, fertile river valleys away from the plateau country, which because of the topography and the marginal soil, was not very good for growing crops.

By the time white men encountered the American Indians of the southeastern United States, they had coalesced into the historic tribes. The Cherokees and Shawnees dominated the region. They did not live on the plateau but frequently hunted the area, using the caves and natural rock shelters as campsites.

The Indians lost their claim to the Southeast region, including the Cumberland Plateau, in several treaties forced on them in the late-1700s and early 1800s. Before and during this period, the descendents of the Europeans who had settled the eastern U.S. began to filter westward. Long hunters were among the first to penetrate the plateau region. They and their descendents eventually settled the Big South Fork country, taking up subsistence farming.

When the first settlers arrived, they lived in the rock shelters the Indians had frequented, closing them off with leaning poles. They soon built pole cabins with mud floors. Eventually, the homes became log cabins with split-log flooring, a loft or second story, and a stone chimney. The people lived by raising crops and livestock and by hunting.

During the period from 1812 to 1865 much saltpeter mining occurred in the rock shelters and caves of the plateau country. An ingredient in gunpowder, saltpeter was a precious commodity during the War of 1812 and the Civil War.

Coal mining and lumbering gradually became important economic activities, contributing to a steady increase in population. The last group of immigrants were the managers and workers needed to run the railroads, coal mines, and lumbering operations of a large industrial development that occurred between 1900 and 1920. The largest operation in the BSF region was the Stearns Coal and Lumber Company, founded in 1902 and eventually commanding many thousands of acres of land. In its peak year, the Stearns Company produced 1,000,000 tons of coal and 18,000,000 board feet of lumber.

With the Depression of the 1930s, the economic prospects of the region declined, never to recover. The coal company towns, the lumber mills, and rail lines were abandoned. Stearns opened its Blue Heron Mine in 1938, and although the mine continued operation until 1962, the end of the economic boom had already been determined.

The camps and settlements were eventually abandoned. Only a few isolated farmsteads and homesites remained. Some coal mining continued, along with oil and gas exploration. But for the most part, the forest and river gorge were left in silence to heal.

By the time the national river and recreation area was authorized in 1974, there were only about forty households of year-round residents still living within the proposed boundaries. Their lands were purchased for the establishment of the park.

These last inhabitants of the Big South Fork watershed had been living primarily on subsistence farms. Growing crops, raising livestock, gathering nuts and berries, hunting, trapping, fishing, and building their own homes were all part of their lifestyle. The farms occasionally included a fenced-off rock shelter as a holding area for livestock.

The rock shelters of the region played a primary role in the human history of the Big South Fork area, from hunting camps through livestock pens to schools and out-of-the-way meeting places for union organizers during the times of mining and lumbering. When you pass through these areas, leave them undisturbed. Digging and rummaging around in the shelters destroys the archaeological record, making it impossible to piece together the history of the Big South Fork.

Plants and Animals

Nearly all the forests of the Cumberland Plateau have been altered by fire, logging, coal mining, and agriculture. But in many places, such as the Big South Fork, second growth timber has reclaimed the land, while small pockets of old-growth forest remain in secluded coves and ravines.

The plateau forest of today consists of two distinct communities. The Uplands Forest inhabits the tableland area, including mountainous regions where overlying beds of soil and stone have yet to erode down to the capstone rock. In these mountains, pine and oak grow on shallow sandy soils along dry ridgetops while on the more moist slopes the mixed pine and oak forest also contains occasional sugar maple, basswood, buckeye, poplar, and beech. The tableland itself is dominated by a mixed oak forest. Along streams and marshy areas, the oaks are interspersed with poplar, red maple, black gum, and sourwood.

While the Uplands Forest is relatively uniform, the plateau gorges are occupied by a more varied Ravine Forest in which several tree species are dominant. The Big South Fork flows through such a complex forest. Distinct climax communities have developed because of differences in elevation, slope exposure, and moisture.

From the edge of the river gorge, thickets of pine, chestnut oak, sourwood, and various shrubs begin the progression of forest communities. The forest on the rim is patrolled by white-tailed deer. The pine warbler and red-breasted nuthatch forage for conifer seeds and insects. Hawks and crows nest in the trees. Hairy woodpeckers, common flickers, and pileated woodpeckers search the trees for insects. The pine seeds are food for the red crossbill, evening grosbeak, bobwhite, turkey, gray squirrel, eastern chipmunk, and white-footed mouse. The eastern cottontail romps in bushy areas.

The massive walls of the gorge stand bare except for a few irregularities in the rock surface that provide footholds for alum root, a few ferns, and small wind-swept pines. Vultures, eastern phoebes, and swallows nest in precarious crevices in the cliff face; an occasional bat clings to the underside of a rock overhang. The red-tailed hawk surveys the gorge from a perch, and the timber rattlesnake and northern copperhead bask in the bright sun.

From the base of the walls, the south-facing slopes descend, clothed in mixed oak communities where turkey, gray squirrel, and opossum are attracted to the mast and thick undergrowth. The wood thrush, hooded warbler, and downy woodpecker frequent the understory, while the red-eyed vireo, scarlet tanager, and tufted-titmouse feed in the canopy.

In the heads of gorges and shaded coves of the north-facing slopes, where understory and groundcover are inhibited, hemlock and rhododendron live in virtual solitude except for a passing deer, bobcat, or fox. Pine and blackpole warblers and the golden-crowned kinglet search for seeds and insects in the canopy.

A forest of sugar maple, beech, poplar, basswood, ash, and buckeye on the low moist slopes provides refuge for gray fox, skunk, and raccoon. The barred owl and red-shouldered hawk search for the smoky shrew, eastern mole, eastern woodrat, white-footed mouse, and eastern chipmunk.

Along the floor of the gorge persists an alluvial forest of sycamore and river birch with wild oats and dense stands of cane; beaver and muskrat, maybe even mink and otter, live in synchronization with the river. The Louisiana waterthrush, spotted sandpiper, and American woodcock explore the wet sand. Recent floods have left debris hanging in the limbs of shrubs and trees along the riverbank.

A gravel and rubble zone possessing a few shrubs edges the river. The strip is inhabited by the bullfrog, southern leopard frog, pickerel frog, water snake, and midland painted turtle. Deer and other large species come to the stream for water as wood ducks paddle by. In the water, riverweed grows on rocks with diatoms and algae in association. These support the zooplankton and aquatic insects that are food for the bluebreast darter, rainbow trout, longear sunfish, and smallmouth bass. Belted kingfishers skim the surface, and green herons lunge for fish and amphibians. Rough-winged swallows, eastern phoebes, and bats feed on the congregating insects.

These plant and animal communities overlap and intermingle to form a single rejuvenated forest.

Out There

There are 300 miles of trails in the national river and recreation area. Some are for hiking only (🏃). Horse trails (∩) may also be used by hikers and mountain bikers. Bike trails (🚲) may be used only by mountain bikers and hikers.

The hiking trails in the Big South Fork are marked with a red arrowhead in a white blaze, with the exceptions of the John Muir Trail, which has a blue silhouette of Muir on a white blaze; the Sheltowee Trace, which has a white or sometimes blue turtle and white diamonds; the Yahoo Falls trails, which have yellow, green, and blue arrowheads in a white blaze; and occasionally a connector trail that has an arrowhead blaze of blue or gray. The blazes are usually spaced close enough that you will see one ahead whenever you begin to wonder if you have strayed from the trail.

Horse trails have the yellow or orange silhouette of a horse's head on a white blaze. Mountain bike trails are blazed with orange arrows on posts or white arrows on brown metal signs; these trails are blazed one-way for safety. Horse riders and mountain bikers should not ride off trail.

Some of the routes described in this book cover old roads and paths that are proposed trails. These have no blazes and no signs, so there is always a chance of getting lost. We have included a few of these trails for experienced hikers and explorers. Please do not attempt these trails if you are new to outdoor recreation. If you travel these trails, pay attention to where you are going so you can at least retrace your steps to get back out if you lose your way. *We expect you to assume full responsibility for knowing where you are going and for not getting lost.*

Trail Descriptions

We begin the trail descriptions with those near the Bandy Creek Visitor Center, which is the first destination for most visitors new to the park. The trail descriptions then spread out from this central location and are grouped by access point. The accompanying maps are designed to help you in finding the access points and the trailheads. The trail numbers correspond to the numbers on the maps.

For each trail description, we give the distance, indicating one-way whenever the trail is not a loop. For those who prefer short outings, we often give the distance to an attraction part way that can be your destination.

We also give a rating of easy, moderate, or difficult. This difficulty rating is based on our subjective judgment of the strenuousness of the trail. While a 10-mile trail would be difficult for anyone not used to hiking, it might be rated easy if it is relatively level, has no creek crossings, and is fairly easy walking. So look not only at the degree of difficulty, but also at the distance.

The elevation gain or loss we give for a trail indicates a difference in elevation between the trail's highest and lowest points. But there could be several ups and downs along the way. We use "elevation change" for the difference between the lowest and highest points on a loop trail, because if you are covering a loop, you will gain and lose the same elevation. We also use "elevation change" when the hike is one-way but the highest or lowest point is along the trail.

We also list cautions, or warnings, about what you might encounter on the trail, such as creek crossings, rocky footing, mudholes, steep climbs, and descents.

Trail connections are included so you may combine several trails for longer outings. To help in making these trail connections, we have also included a trail index.

Then after briefly mentioning the trail's attractions and giving directions to the trailhead, we describe what you'll encounter along the trail. The mileages given in the descriptions are almost always cumulative. If you want to hike or ride the trail in the reverse direction from our description, it will probably be helpful if you calculate the reverse mileages.

Preparations

Even if you are out for only a short time, you should wear walking shoes or boots. Carry along water, a lunch or snacks, rain gear, a first aid kit, and a map and compass; and just in case you get lost or injured, bring along extra clothes, a knife, a flashlight, a lighter or waterproof matches plus some firestarter, and a plastic sheet or emergency blanket.

If you are backpacking or horse or bike camping, you'll need everything for surviving in the open overnight and for however many days you choose to be out. If you are inexperienced, the park rangers or your local outfitters can give advice on the equipment needed.

Once at the trailhead, you should be able to find your way by using our descriptions and the signs at most trail junctions. Always let someone know where you are going. If you get lost, do not leave the trail.

You'll need to check the topographical maps that cover your area. Our maps are designed to help you with the general route and trail connections; they do not provide for detailed navigating. At the minimum, you should have along a trail map that gives you an overall view of the park and the trail connections, available at the Visitor Center.

Precautions

Be especially careful climbing on rocks, hiking or riding along the edge of bluffs, crossing streams, and passing near the river. Do not climb on waterfalls. *We expect you to take responsibility for your own safety, keeping in mind that being in a wilderness setting far from medical attention is an inherently hazardous activity.* It is best to travel with someone; if one of you is hurt, the other can care for the injured and go for help.

The northern copperhead and the timber rattler live here; always watch where you put your feet and hands, and give snakes a wide berth. On warm spring and summer days, the gnats, black flies, and mosquitoes can be a bother, so carry along insect repellant. Before starting off on a hike, spray your shoetops, socks, legs, and pants with repellant to discourage ticks; one type, the deer tick, can transmit a spirochete that causes Lyme disease. And remember to check yourself after a hike.

Stream crossings can be easy or difficult. After a heavy rain, a stream can be swollen with rushing water. Do not attempt to cross such a stream unless you are sure you can make it. If you cannot see the bottom, you should probably not try to ford.

In cold and wet weather, you face the danger of hypothermia. The symptoms are uncontrolled shivering, slurred speech, memory lapse, stumbling, fumbling hands, and drowsiness. If you are wet and cold, get under some shelter, change into dry clothes, and drink warm fluids. Get in a sleeping bag, if available. To prevent hypothermia, stay dry, eat even if you are not hungry, and drink water even when you are not thirsty.

Finally, hunting is allowed in the park, subject to the regulations of the states of Kentucky and Tennessee. Check at the Visitor Center or with any ranger for whether hunting is going on; always wear bright clothing during hunting seasons.

Camping

The Bandy Creek Campground is located in the Tennessee portion of the park near the Visitor Center, north of TN297 on the west side of the river. The smaller Blue Heron Campground is in the Kentucky portion of the park, north of Mine 18 Road on the way to the Blue Heron Mining Community on the east side of the river. A new equestrian camp is located at Station Camp East on the Station Camp Road in Tennessee, and one is under construction near the Bear Creek Scenic Area off KY742 in Kentucky. These are all fee campgrounds. There's also primitive camping at Alum Ford at the end of KY700 at the northern end of the park.

If you plan to camp in the backcountry, let a ranger know your plans, even though registration is not required. You may camp virtually anywhere, but set up at least 25 feet from trails, gravel and dirt roads, rock shelters, the gorge rim, and major geologic and historic features, at least 100 feet from streams and paved roads, and at least 200 feet from trailheads, parking lots, and cemeteries. You may use only dead and down timber for campfires. Hang your food at night to keep it away from animals.

Boil all water in the backcountry at least one minute before drinking to destroy bacteria and other microorganisms, including Giardia, a flagellate protozoan causing an intestinal disorder called "Giardiasis." Filters and water purifying tablets can be used, but ask your supplier for ones that indeed remove Giardia.

Bury your waste at least six inches deep and at least 100 feet away from trails, water sources, and campsites. Pack out all trash and litter.

Short Walks

Found throughout the national river and recreation area, short walks provide quick and usually easy access to various attractions. If you have only a brief time to spend in the park or are a beginner to hiking, you'll get a taste of what's waiting for you by taking one or two of these short walks.

The 0.4-mile *Riverwalk* at Leatherwood Ford on TN297 leads along the shore of the river. Start at the information gazebo and take the path and steps down toward the old Leatherwood Ford Bridge and turn right on the paved walkway. The trail includes boardwalks, benches, and bridges scattered among patches of sand, river rock, and alluvial forest. The boardwalks and platforms are built so low to the water they are often submerged when the river is at flood stage; so at high water, use caution walking along the river.

The 0.1-mile *East Rim Overlook Trail,* from the end of the East Rim Overlook Road across from the park headquarters on TN297, takes you down a paved walkway to a platform view of the Big South Fork Gorge.

The 0.4-mile *Confluence Trail* takes you down to the confluence of the New and Clear Fork Rivers that create the Big South Fork. At 2.7 miles south of Oneida on US27 turn west on the road to the airport. Cross a bridge over the railroad line and immediately turn left. At 3.8 miles turn right, and then at 4.8 miles turn left onto a graveled road that passes behind the Scott County Memorial Airport. At 7.5 miles keep left at a fork. You'll cross the boundary into the park at 7.9 miles and then reach the end of the road and parking at 8.8 miles. Walk the gated road to the right, which leads down to the confluence.

The 0.4-mile *Yamacraw Loop* drops beside a tumbling stream and passes along the river shore. From Stearns, take KY92 west to the crossing of the Big South Fork and turn right into the Yamacraw Day Use Area just before the Yamacraw Bridge. The loop first follows the Sheltowee Trace north but soon turns left off the Trace to drop to the edge of the river. You'll then follow an old dirt road that circles back under the highway bridge and ascends to meet the other end of the parking area.

The 0.1-mile *Devils Jump Overlook Trail* leads to a broad platform at the gorge rim and a view of the Devils Jump Rapids in the river far below. Turn west on the Overlooks Road off the Mine 18 Road on the way to the Blue Heron Community. At 1.1 miles, you'll see the parking area for the overlook on the left.

At the end of the Overlooks Road, 0.3 mile beyond the Devils Jump Overlook, you'll find a turnaround loop and parking for the 0.2-mile *Blue Heron Overlook Trail* that leads to a panoramic overlook of the gorge. Just before reaching the overlook, you'll see a trail to the right that has a blue arrow blaze. This trail descends the bluff in a series of stairs to connect with the Blue Heron Loop in 0.1 mile.

At the Blue Heron Mining Community, you can walk the *Blue Heron Exhibit Trail* from the Depot/Museum. The 0.2-mile Loop A of the trail begins across the road from the Depot and leads by exhibits and then crosses the road to loop back to the Depot. On the 0.3-mile Loop B to the right of the Depot, you'll pass several of the interpretive buildings, the Mine 18 entrance, the east end of the tipple bridge, and a side trail blazed with a gray arrow that leads 0.2 mile along the old tramroad to the former powder magazine.

To get to the 0.2-mile *Bear Creek Overlook Trail*, turn south off the Mine 18 Road that leads down to Blue Heron at a sign directing you to the Bear Creek Scenic Area, and follow additional signs 3.5 miles to the scenic area. From the parking area the trail leads through an abandoned field and then the woods to a platform overlook offering a sweeping view of the BSF Gorge.

The 0.2-mile *Dick Gap Overlook Trail* follows a wide graveled path from the end of Dick Gap Road to the park's newest overlook. From the west side of the Yamacraw Bridge on KY92, turn south on KY1363 and then after 2.3 miles, turn left on Beech Grove Road. Along the way it becomes a single track and eventually gravel; watch for oncoming traffic. At 4 miles from the turn onto Beech Grove Road, you'll pass the Beech Grove Baptist Church on the left; then just beyond, turn left on the Waters Cemetery Road. In a half mile turn left on Dick Gap Road. You'll reach the end of the road in another mile; down to your left you'll see the trail to the overlook, which gives a good view of the Blue Heron Mining Community across the river.

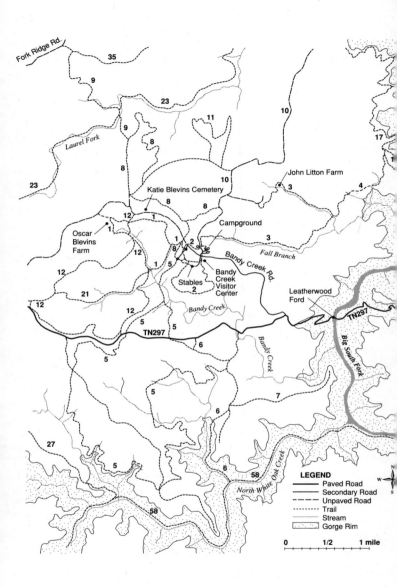

Map 3. Bandy Creek
18

⬆ Oscar Blevins Farm Loop ⅄⅄

3.6 miles
Easy
Elevation change: 180 ft.
Cautions: Creek crossings, stairs
Connections: Bandy Creek Campground Loop ⅄⅄, North
Bandy Creek Trail ∩, West Entrance Trail ⅄⅄,
Collier Ridge Loop ⊶

Attractions: Stands of tall laurel and rhododendron line the trail along Bandy Creek on the way to the Oscar Blevins Farm.

Trailhead: If visiting the BSFNRRA for the first time, you'll likely want to start at the Visitor Center at Bandy Creek. In the Tennessee portion of the park, on the west side of the river on TN297, turn north on Bandy Creek Road. If you are coming from the west, the turn is just before the road drops into the river gorge. Coming from the east, you must descend into the gorge, cross the river on the bridge at Leatherwood Ford, and travel up the other side to get to the turnoff. After making the turn, go 1.8 miles to reach the Visitor Center on the left. A campground lies on the right. At 0.2 mile farther up the road, turn left and you'll find parking for the Bandy Creek Trailhead on the right.

Description: The Oscar Blevins Farm Loop heads straight into the woods while the Bandy Creek Campground Loop crosses the path at the trailhead. The Blevins Loop begins as a gravel path and with a small footbridge over a low area. Numbered posts correspond to a printed guide you can get at the Visitor Center.

At 0.1 mile you'll cross the North Bandy Creek Trail. Then a footbridge near the West Bandy Creek Road takes you over a creek just before encountering the actual loop at 0.2 mile. The best approach is to hike the loop clockwise, to the left.

The trail descends gradually, following the small creek, a tributary of Bandy Creek that may be dry at times. You'll enter a miniature gorge with the creek cascading down the rock bluff and spilling over a ledge just at a wooden platform where you must step down a wooden stairway. Soon after, you'll cross the boundary into Scott State Forest, an inholding still owned by the state of Tennessee. The trail then passes through stands of laurel and at 0.5 mile crosses a footbridge over a wet area.

At 0.7 mile, a side trail up to the right leads to Muleshoe Rockshelter, where old mule shoes have been found. At 1.0 mile, you'll cross the north branch of Bandy Creek on a bridge; an early homestead was abandoned in the area, and the word "abandoned" was shortened to "banded," which was then corrupted to "bandy." On the other side of the creek, you'll encounter a junction with the West Entrance Trail that leads left. Stay straight.

You'll soon merge with a roadbed that is part of the Collier Ridge Bike Loop; the two trails coincide along the roadway, which was the access for several farms in the area. You'll pass the site of the old farmstead of Billie Blevins; fields, an old chicken coop, and the foundation of a house remain. The trail crosses King Branch. At 1.6 miles, a trail up to the left is the return portion of the bike loop. Soon after, the hiking trail bears left, leaving the bike trail, and follows another old road to cross Bandy Creek again on a bridge at 1.7 miles.

As you approach the site of the Oscar Blevins farm, you'll pass the remains of a split-rail fence. Where you cross a footbridge, an abandoned root cellar sits on the left. At 2.0 miles, you'll stand in front of the frame house that was the home of Oscar and Ermon Blevins. You can explore the farmsite, which to the rear includes a large barn flanked by a hog shed, chicken coop, corn crib, and a log house built in 1879. The farm, a historic site, is typical of early 20th century homesteads.

In front of the house, a road leads out to West Bandy Creek Road. Turn right on a footpath to continue the hiking loop. After a couple of bridges, you'll cross the upper end of the Collier Ridge Loop at 2.5 miles. You'll cross another footbridge and then at 2.8 miles reach the location of interpretive post #20; an overgrown side path here leads 50 yards up to the West Bandy Creek Road across from the Lora Blevins House and the Katie Blevins Cemetery. Oscar Blevins is buried there.

Crossing three boardwalks over drainages and swinging through the head of a hollow, you'll close the loop at 3.4 miles. Then return along the connector to the trailhead.

1879 Farmhouse

⓶ Bandy Creek
Campground Loop 🚶🚶

2.3 miles
Easy
Elevation change: 80 ft.
Cautions: Footbridges slippery in wet weather
Connections: Oscar Blevins Farm Loop 🚶🚶, Duncan Hollow
Trail ∩, John Litton Farm Loop 🚶🚶, N. Bandy Creek Trail ∩

Attractions: This loop introduces you to the facilities at Bandy Creek and to the Uplands Forest.

Trailhead: Follow the directions in Trail #1 to the Bandy Creek Trailhead. You may also begin the Loop at the Visitor Center.

Description: From the trailhead, take the path to the right. You'll cross a boardwalk over a low area, pass under a powerline, and at 0.1 mile cross the Bandy Creek Road where the pavement gives way to gravel; the graveled section to the left is referred to as the "West Bandy Creek Road." The trail curves to the right below campsites to then pass behind the volleyball court and swimming pool and cross Duncan Hollow Road at 0.4 mile. At the trailhead for the John Litton Farm Loop, walk a few feet up that trail to turn right and pass behind the campfire circle. You'll emerge on a road within the campground. Bear right along roads toward the campground entrance. Behind the check-in kiosk, take a path to the left that crosses the Bandy Creek Road and enters the Visitor Center parking area at 0.7 mile.

Head straight into the woods to walk through an Uplands Forest of mixed pine and oak. You'll loop around the horse stables complex. At 1.9 miles, the path crosses the North Bandy Creek Trail leading from the stables to the Bandy Creek Equestrian Trailhead. You'll emerge to pass a pond and turn left toward the amphitheater; then turn right on a path. You'll cross a couple of boardwalks and reach a junction with a path to the equestrian trailhead to the left. Staying straight, you'll cross the trailhead road and circle right to arrive back at the trailhead at 2.3 miles.

③ John Litton Farm Loop 👫

5.9 miles
Easy to Moderate
Elevation change: 300 ft.
Cautions: Stairway, ladder, footbridges
Connections: Bandy Creek Campground Loop 👫, Fall Branch
Trail 👫, Duncan Hollow Trail ∩, Duncan Hollow Loop 🚲,
Katie Trail ∩

Attractions: This loop takes you by terraced rock bluffs and Fall
Branch Falls en route to the John Litton Farm historic site.

Trailhead: Across from the Bandy Creek Visitor Center, drive
into the campground and bear left to park at the swimming pool;
you'll see the trailhead just as Duncan Hollow Road enters the
woods. You may also take the Bandy Creek Campground Loop
0.4-mile to the right from the Bandy Creek Trailhead.

Description: Hike the trail counterclockwise for the best
approach. The trail begins as a graveled path; immediately you'll
pass a path to the right that leads to the campground campfire
circle. The trail then parallels Duncan Hollow Road to the left
but soon swings right and crosses a stream on footbridge at 0.2
mile before leading into a fragrant pine and laurel forest.

Soon you'll hear Fall Branch as the trail switches back and
drops toward the creek on your right. You'll skirt sandstone
shelves on your left with hemlocks balanced at the edge. Wooden
steps and then a ladder at 0.6 mile and switchbacks take you past
dripping rock overhangs and gradually drop you into a carpet of
ferns beside the creek.

The trail passes rock bluffs and makes several side stream
crossings over footbridges. You'll encounter the Scott State Forest
boundary and then cross under a power line. At 1.9 miles you'll
come to Fall Branch Falls. The creek pours off a rock shelf and
drops ten feet into a green pool—a perfect spot for lunch, re-
laxing, or maybe even a splash in the pool.

From here the trail climbs away from Fall Branch through

a young pine grove. Along the way, watch for climbing fern, so thick at one location on both sides of the trail it reminded us of kudzu. At 2.8 miles, take the bridge across the North Fork of Fall Branch, and you'll come to a junction with the Fall Branch Trail to the right. To stay with the John Litton Farm Loop, turn left. You'll cross several small side streams, some on footbridges; others you just step over. The trail eventually merges with an old roadbed leading to the farm at 3.7 miles.

The John Litton Farm sits in a cove to the left, including the house John Litton built around 1900. The Litton Farm is also called the General Slaven Farm, "General" was his name, not a title. The Slavens added a frame addition and porches to the original cabin.

The trail curves left over an earthen dam holding back blackberry bushes and a stream-fed pond still alive with fish. You'll cross a footbridge over the spillway for the pond and then descend to a junction with an old road that has come down from the Duncan Hollow Road. To the left sits a side-opening English barn built by John Litton. The trail turns to the left beside the barn on another old roadway. You'll cross a bridge over the North Fork and soon turn right to begin a climb away from the farm. The ascent includes several switchbacks and a set of stairs.

At 4.5 miles the trail joins a roadbed leading to a clearing. Turn right to stay along the edge of the woods. You'll pass an old farmsite up to the left and then cross a footbridge over a drainage to merge with an old road to the right. You'll reach a junction with the graveled road at 4.8 miles that leads to the farm; it's gated farther down to prevent vehicle access. Turn left to complete the loop. A proposed rerouting will eventually take the hiking trail off this road to loop back through the woods.

Continue straight to cross the meandering boundary of Scott State Forest. At 5.0 miles, you'll reach a junction with the Duncan Hollow Road. The Duncan Hollow Trail and the Duncan Hollow Loop follow this road to the right. Turn left on the road. You'll pass under a powerline.

At 5.6 miles the Katie Trail leads to the west. Stay straight on the road to cross the state forest boundary once more and complete the loop at 5.9 miles.

4 Fall Branch Trail 👫

1.9 miles one-way
Easy
Elevation gain: 150 ft.
Cautions: None
Connections: John Litton Farm Loop 👫, John Muir Trail 👫

Attractions: This trail serves to connect the farm loop with the JMT while passing by a rock shelter and isolated streams.

Trailhead: The trail begins at 2.8 miles counterclockwise along the John Litton Farm Loop. See Trail #3 for details.

Description: From the junction with the John Litton Farm Loop, the trail heads downstream along the North Fork of Fall Branch. At 0.1 mile, the trail threads a rock passageway, curves left, and crosses a footbridge over a small drainage to pass in front of a deep rock shelter. You'll climb steps along the rock wall and pass a smaller hole in the wall before making switchbacks left and right to climb above the rock shelter.

You'll continue to climb with other switchbacks, eventually joining an old roadbed. At 0.3 mile, you'll cross the boundary leaving Scott State Forest. You'll then drop through a cove and pass an old roadway up to the left. At 0.8 mile, you'll cross a small footbridge at an old roadway going downhill to the right.

The trail curves left up a cove and drops to a bridge over the upper end of the cove at 1.2 miles. You'll turn right after the bridge and begin an ascent with switchbacks left and right. After swinging through a couple more coves, watch for a left turn at 1.5 miles. Then watch for a right turn as you descend to a bridge over a tributary of Fall Branch at 1.8 miles; this is the last source of water for some time.

After the bridge, the trail turns left and begins an ascent with several switchbacks to connect with the John Muir Trail at 1.9 miles. This section of the JMT is also part of the Grand Gap Loop; see Trail #16 for details.

⑤ South Bandy Creek Trail/ North White Oak Loop ∩

16.1 miles
Moderate
Elevation change: 200 ft.
Cautions: Creek crossings, sandy patches
Connections: North Bandy Creek Trail ∩,
Leatherwood Overlook Trail ∩, Coyle Branch Trail ∩,
Gar Blevins Trail ∩, Groom Branch Trail ∩

Attractions: This popular horse trail circles through the Uplands Forest of the plateau tableland.

Trailhead: You can begin this trail from the Bandy Creek Equestrian Trailhead that is just beyond the hiking trailhead on the side road off Bandy Creek Road; follow the directions in Trail #1. But if you're walking or biking and want to avoid some of the horse traffic and the frequent mudholes on the first section from the trailhead down to the highway, there's access off TN297. Head west on TN297 from the junction of the Bandy Creek Road into the Visitor Center. The highway dips to cross Bandy Creek. At 1.2 miles turn left on a side road that's paved for the first few yards; park here so you do not block the road. Follow the dirt road into the woods and you'll connect with the loop trail in 0.1 mile.

Description: At the Bandy Creek Equestrian Trailhead, the North Bandy Creek Trail leads left to the stables in 0.3 mile where many horse riders begin their rides; this trail continues right to connect with horse trails to the north. Head straight through the Loop F Corral Area to begin this ride. Loop F was once a campsite but is now day-use only.

You'll descend on the South Bandy Creek Trail. After making a switchback right, you'll ford Bandy Creek at 0.5 mile. From here on you'll run into some serious mudholes in wet weather, unless the trail has been improved. At 0.7 mile, you'll reach the junction with the North White Oak Loop. We usually cover the trail clockwise, so stay left.

The trail crosses a streambed on a footbridge and then switch-backs left down to cross a small creek on a bridge at 1.0 mile. You'll ascend to a crossing of TN297 at 1.7 miles. On the other side, turn left to parallel the highway. At 1.9 miles, you'll emerge into an open area where there is additional access off TN297. Stay with the road straight ahead. At 2.1 miles, a side road right leads down to a pond. You'll then reach a junction at 2.2 miles where it's 0.1 mile left up to our recommended parking for hikers and mountain bikers on TN297. If you begin and end there, you'll trim about 3 miles from the route.

Continue straight on the old road. You'll pass open fields on the right and then to the left. The road is mostly hard-packed gravel.

At 2.7 miles you'll connect with the old White Pine Road and bear right; to the left, the old roadway leads out to TN297 after fording Bandy Creek. Then at 2.8 miles, you'll reach a junction with the White Pine Road continuing straight for access to the Leatherwood Overlook and Coyle Branch Trails. The North White Oak Loop turns right off the road. Making the right turn, you'll drop off the road through a wet area and ascend to pass through a pine woods with large patches of ground cedar, fol-lowing the trace of an old road. Mountain bikers should watch for patches of sand where the bikes lose traction now that you're off the road.

You'll cross a small stream at 3.2 miles and soon after cross the boundary into Scott State Forest. As the trail meanders through the woods, it crosses and recrosses the boundary several times.

At 4.2 miles, you'll cross an earth-filled causeway that traverses a wet area. The trail passes through posts that limit ve-hicle access at 4.9 miles; soon after, you'll pass an old road com-ing down from the right and pass through posts on the other side. The trail then crosses the shallow Coyle Branch of North White Oak Creek and bears left. At 5.4 miles bear left where another old road joins on the right.

You'll ford the West Fork of Coyle Branch at 5.8 miles where the stream is undercutting a low rock bluff to the right. The trail then heads downstream along the creek's drainage; you'll fre-quently swing right to cross the drainages of side streams. Watch for a small waterfall on one of these at 6.6 miles.

The trail crosses an old road at 7.8 miles and then reaches a junction at 8.0 miles. To the right the Gar Blevins Trail cuts through the middle of the loop to emerge on TN297. To the left is the North White Oak Overlook Trail that leads 1.6 miles out to an overlook of North White Oak Creek, which you may want to see before going on. Stay straight to continue the loop.

At 9.5 miles, you'll cross an old road that is a fork off the Gar Blevins Trail up to the right. To the left, the old road gets overgrown. Continuing on the loop trail, you'll pass large rocks up to the right and at 10.4 miles cross a footbridge over a bottom area thick with cinnamon fern. The trail soon crosses a bridge over a creekbed with more fern.

At 11.3 miles, you'll cross a shallow creek that flows across the path and then cross the main creek on a bridge and soon another footbridge over a small stream. At 11.9 miles, the path crosses a creek on a bridge; again notice the stands of cinnamon fern downstream. You'll soon cross a footbridge over a low area.

Then at 12.9 miles the trail once again crosses the Gar Blevins Trail. At 13.2 miles, you'll reach a junction with the Groom Branch Trail to the left that recrosses the Gar Blevins Trail in 70 yards and heads west toward the Cumberland Valley Trailhead. At 14.2 miles, you'll pass an old road to the left; keep straight, cross the Scott State Forest boundary and then another old road, and emerge on TN297 at 14.6 miles. If you started at the Bandy Creek Equestrian Trailhead, cross the road and continue on the horse trail. You'll descend to close the loop at 15.4 miles. Turning left, you'll ascend back to the trailhead at 16.1 miles, fording Bandy Creek again along the way.

But for hikers and mountain bikers who started the loop at the parking on TN297, turn right when you reach the highway and walk or bike down the road 0.5 mile to pick up the horse trail again, turning right off the road and proceeding another 0.5 mile to the junction with the road up to the parking for a loop total of 13.5 miles.

⑥ Coyle Branch Trail ∩

2.8 miles one-way
Difficult
Elevation loss: 550 ft.
Cautions: Sandy patches, steep rocky descent
Connections: North White Oak Loop ∩, Leatherwood
Overlook Trail ∩, O&W Railbed ∩ 🚴

Attractions: This trail provides access to the O&W Railbed from the Bandy Creek area.

Trailhead: From the turnoff for the Bandy Creek Visitor Center, continue west on TN297. At 0.6 mile, just past the White Pine United Baptist Church and just before TN297 crosses Bandy Creek, you'll pass White Pine Road on the left that provides unofficial access to the Coyle Branch Trail. Continue west on TN297 another 0.6 mile and turn in a side road on the left that's the Burke Farm Road and park so you do not block the road. This is also the alternative access for hikers and mountain bike riders described for the North White Oak Loop. With a horse trailer, you may want to begin at the Bandy Creek Equestrian Trailhead or the Bandy Creek Stables.

Description: At 0.1 mile down this road, you'll connect with the North White Oak Loop and turn left to a junction with the old White Pine Road to the left at 0.6 mile.

From this junction, head south, to the right, on the North White Oak Loop. At 0.7 mile, the loop turns off to the right. Stay straight on the road. You'll pass an old road to the left and at 1.1 miles reach a junction with a road to the left that takes you to the Leatherwood Overlook. Stay straight to continue on the Coyle Branch Trail.

At 1.2 miles, you'll reach a fork, with the Coyle Branch Road right and the White Pine Road continuing left. Here you can take a side excursion of 0.7 mile on the White Pine Road, which is graveled until it emerges into the long Duvall Fields that's an agricultural lease area. At the far end of the fields, you can walk a path that leads down through the woods to an overlook of the Coyle Branch Gorge.

Back at the fork, bear right off the White Pine Road onto the Coyle Branch Road. You'll soon reach the end of the access for motorized vehicles and begin a steep rocky descent with paths around deep ruts in the old roadbed. At 1.5 miles, you'll pass the trace of an old road up to the left and, soon after, drop below the rock bluff to an overhang; below to your right you'll see or hear Coyle Branch. You'll now parallel the creek downstream.

After a level stretch, you'll round a rock bluff to the left and descend again to cross a small drainage and thread a rock passageway at 1.7 miles. At 2.0 miles, you'll drop down a two-foot rock ledge and continue your descent, passing mudholes along the way if there have been recent rains.

At 2.8 miles, the trail reaches a junction with the old O&W Railbed that runs along North White Oak Creek; just to the right, Coyle Branch joins North White Oak Creek. At this writing, the old railbed is open to motorized vehicles. You can turn left on the railbed to get to a ford of North White Oak Creek and the O&W Bridge beyond. Turning right, you can connect with the Gernt Trail or continue on to the Zenith area. Or you can retrace your route back to TN297.

7 Leatherwood Overlook Trail ∩

1.9 miles one-way
Easy
Mostly level
Cautions: None
Connections: Coyle Branch Trail ∩

Attractions: This side trail takes you out to an overlook of Leatherwood Ford.

Trailhead: You can access this trail from the North White Oak Loop. At 2.8 miles along the North White Oak Loop, continue straight on the old White Pine Road as the loop turns off right. In another 0.5 mile, turn left on the Leatherwood Overlook Trail as the Coyle Branch Trail continues straight.

Description: Turning left on the Leatherwood Overlook Trail, you'll pass old roads to the right and left and then pass through the Terry/Thompson Fields, an agricultural lease area. You'll see a pond to your right in the field. At 1.3 miles you'll reach the woodline at a junction; the road continues to the right while the trail to the overlook goes straight. If you were to stay on the road, you'd reach the end of vehicle access in 0.3 mile. If you're a hiker skilled at exploring unmarked trails, you can continue on the trace of the old road to curve left and descend steeply, passing below Leatherwood Overlook and reaching a level with the river at the mouth of Bandy Creek. You can then ford the creek and continue on an overgrown path and emerge on TN297 at Leatherwood Ford. This route is not recommended for horses, mountain bikes, or inexperienced hikers.

Continuing toward the overlook from the junction at the end of the field, you'll travel along the trail on old roadway. You'll descend to hitching rails at 1.8 miles and walk out to the overlook at 1.9 miles. You'll have a view of the river and the Leatherwood Ford Bridge; to the left lies the Bandy Creek Gorge.

Leatherwood Overlook

⑧ North Bandy Creek Trail/ Katie Trail/Jacks Ridge Loop ∩

8.2 miles
Easy
Elevation change: 200 ft.
Cautions: None
Connections: South Bandy Creek Trail ∩, North White Oak
Loop ∩, By-Pass Trail ∩, Black House Branch Trail ∩

Attractions: You'll have a pleasant horse ride with sandy tread.

Trailhead: Follow the directions in Trail #5 to the Bandy Creek Equestrian Trailhead. No-bicycle use is proposed for this route; long patches of deep sand make it not a good ride for bikes.

Description: To get to the Jacks Ridge Loop, you must first head north on the North Bandy Creek Trail from the trailhead; part of this trail leads east from the trailhead to the stables where you may also begin the ride. South from the trailhead, you'll see the South Bandy Creek Trail that leads to the North White Oak Loop.

On the North Bandy Creek Trail, at 0.3 mile, you'll cross the Oscar Blevins Farm Loop hiking trail. Then at 0.4 mile you'll cross the graveled West Bandy Creek Road and reach a junction with the Katie Trail at 0.6 mile. Right on this trail takes you to the Duncan Hollow Road in 0.4 mile. Turn left.

You'll pass through an open area; stay with the wide main trail where paths lead off to the right that connect with By-Pass Road. You may still see many pine trees down from the winter freeze of '94. The last time we rode the trail a red fox romped down the path in front of us before veering off into the woods. At 1.3 miles, you'll cross a low area on a short causeway and then emerge into another open area that's at a distance behind the Lora Blevins House and the Katie Blevins Cemetery.

At 1.5 miles, you'll step over a small creek as the trail turns left to pass through another open area. You'll then reach a junction with the Jacks Ridge Loop at 2.0 miles. Stay straight. Just beyond, you'll cross By-Pass Road that comes down from Jacks

North Bandy Creek Trail

Ridge Road to the left; a sign there calls it "Duncan Hollow Road" because By-Pass Road connects with the Duncan Hollow Road to the east. You'll complete the Jacks Ridge Loop by returning along the By-Pass Road from the right.

Beyond this crossing of By-Pass Road, the trail joins Jacks Ridge Road. Back to the left, you can reach West Bandy Creek Road in 0.1 mile, where you can also access the Jacks Ridge Loop; there's parking at the road junction for one vehicle.

As you continue down the Jacks Ridge Road, you'll pass a couple of old roads to the right and reach a junction at 2.7 miles. To the left the Black House Branch Trail follows an old road down to a ford of Laurel Fork and then heads north toward Charit Creek Lodge. Stay straight at this junction to continue the loop.

You'll soon bear left off the old roadbed; it's here that the road ends for motorized vehicles. The trail now follows a path through the woods, dotted with blooming mountain laurel in May and early June. At 3.3 miles, you'll pass under a powerline and turn left up the cleared area to a distant view of the Laurel Fork Gorge before turning to the right back into the woods.

After the trail meanders through the woods, it passes back under the powerline at 4.0 miles. At 4.6 miles, you'll cross a bridge over a small creek and then a couple of short causeways and emerge onto the end of an old road at 5.2 miles. Turn right to connect with another road and turn right. The trail veers left off this road at 5.5 miles.

At 6.1 miles, the trail connects with By-Pass Road. This is a designated horse trail that to the left connects with Duncan Hollow Road in 2.2 miles. At the junction of the Jacks Ridge Loop with By-Pass Road, turn right to close the loop at 6.2 miles. It's then 2.0 miles back along the Katie Trail and the North Bandy Creek Trail to the Bandy Creek Equestrian Trailhead.

⑨ Black House Branch Trail ∩

2.0 miles one-way
Moderate
Elevation change: 360 ft.
Cautions: Creek fords, steep descent and ascent
Connections: Jacks Ridge Loop ∩, Laurel Fork Creek Trail 🐾,
Fork Ridge Trail ∩, Charit Creek Lodge Trail ∩

Attractions: Traditionally called the "Charit Creek Lodge Trail," this horse trail provides access from the Bandy Creek area to the Middle Creek area and Charit Creek Lodge to the northwest.

Trailhead: Follow the directions in Trail #8 from the Bandy Creek Equestrian Trailhead north along the North Bandy Creek Trail and then the Katie Trail and the Jacks Ridge Loop to the junction with the Black House Branch Trail at 2.7 miles. This junction can also be accessed along the Jacks Ridge Road, which can be reached by continuing north on the West Bandy Creek Road 1.1 miles from the turnoff for the Bandy Creek trailheads. Jacks Ridge Road is the dirt road to the right just after you cross the county line. The road is open to vehicles for 0.8 mile to a parking area at the beginning of the Black House Branch Trail; this road should probably be tried only with four-wheel drive because of the deep sand and occasional mudholes. There's room for a vehicle to park beside West Bandy Creek Road if you want to walk or ride from the beginning of the Jacks Ridge Road.

Description: From the parking area at the junction of the Black House Branch Trail with the Jacks Ridge Loop/Road, head left down the side road. You'll see a bar gate restricting vehicle access; make your way around the gate and continue down the steep graveled road. At 0.1 mile, notice up to your right a small rock shelter as you begin to drop below the sandstone bluff of Laurel Fork Gorge.

The road passes a massive block of stone that has separated from the rim at 0.2 mile. At 0.3 mile the road curves right in its descent and finally curves left to a ford of the Laurel Fork of

Station Camp Creek at 0.4 mile; hikers may find it a little more shallow upstream. Just before the ford, you'll see a camping spot on the left.

Across the creek, you'll connect with the Laurel Fork Creek Trail for hikers, which to the left leads toward the West Entrance Trailhead. You'll see several trail signs, more confusing than helpful because they do not distinguish between horse and hiking trails; so just ignore them all and turn right on the road, which is multiple-use for horses and hikers. At 0.5 mile, you'll reach a junction with the Laurel Fork Creek Trail turning off to the right; this is a hiking trail and not open to horses. Stay with the road to the left to keep on the Black House Branch Trail; the road is mostly hard-packed gravel, but you'll find occasional mudholes to slog through.

At 0.6 mile, the road fords Black House Branch on its way to join Laurel Fork; to the left notice the large rock overhanging the water. You'll ford the branch twice more at 0.7 mile and 0.8 mile. At 0.9 mile, you'll pass through a more open area, and then the road curves to the right uphill. You'll switchback left and right as you make the ascent out of the Laurel Fork Gorge.

At 1.4 miles the road skirts a clearing for a powerline and continues up past a gate to the top of the plateau at 1.5 miles. Through the woods, you'll emerge in the open and pass under the powerline at 1.7 miles. Reentering the woods, you'll see an old roadway joins the main road on the right. You'll then reach a junction with a road at 2.0 miles that is the Fork Ridge Trail. To the left, it's 0.1 mile out to Fork Ridge Road and then right to the trails down to Charit Creek Lodge. To the right, the Fork Ridge Trail heads toward the confluence of Laurel Fork and Station Camp Creek.

1️⃣0️⃣ **Duncan Hollow Trail** ∩

5.7 miles one-way
Moderate
Elevation loss: 720 ft.
Cautions: Steep rocky descent, creek ford, motorized vehicles
Connections: John Litton Farm Loop 🐾, Katie Trail ∩,
By-Pass Trail ∩, Duncan Hollow Loop 🚲, Laurel Fork Creek
Trail 🐾, Fork Ridge Trail ∩, John Muir Trail 🐾,
Station Camp Creek Trail ∩

Attractions: This trail gives access to the Station Camp Creek area and can be combined with the Black House Branch Trail and the Station Camp Creek Trail or Fork Ridge Trail to make a loop for horse riders and mountain bikers.

Trailhead: Hikers and mountain bikers follow the directions in Trail #3 to the John Litton Farm Loop Trailhead. Horse riders follow the directions in Trail #8 along the North Bandy Creek Trail and right on the Katie Trail.

Description: From the swimming pool parking area, hikers and bikers head down the graveled Duncan Hollow Road. The Duncan Hollow Trail follows the road, which is open to vehicles for the first 4.2 miles and can be managed by passenger cars for most of its length before you run into mudholes and soft sand. Immediately, you'll pass the John Litton Farm Loop, which leads off to the right.

You'll cross the Scott State Forest boundary and reach a junction with the Katie Trail merging from the left at 0.3 mile; this is the location for horse riders to access the Duncan Hollow Trail. At 0.9 mile, you'll pass under a powerline and reach a fork. The road to the right leads toward the John Litton Farm and is part of the farm loop. Stay left at the fork.

At 1.2 miles, you'll pass By-Pass Road on the left that connects with the Jacks Ridge Loop. The Duncan Hollow Bike Loop, which has also been following the road, turns left here to make its loop route. Stay straight at this junction. You'll pass a couple of dirt roads to the right and at 2.7 miles enter an open area of old fields; notice the housesite to the left with blocks of stone from the chimney still piled in the center. Continuing on the road, you'll reenter the woods, pass the traces of old roads to the left and right, and reach the end of vehicle access at 4.2 miles.

A proposal calls for rerouting the trail from here to a less steep descent into the Laurel Fork Gorge. But for the time being, stay straight on the old roadway as it begins its descent. A path to the right parallels the road; at 4.4 miles this path rejoins the old road. Soon after, a small stream flows across the trail in wet weather. At 4.5 miles the trail drops below the rock bluff and then passes a rock shelter up to the right.

You'll then pass through a series of switchbacks as the trail, following the old roadway, makes a steep, rocky, often muddy descent to a ford of Laurel Fork Creek at 5.4 miles. Here the Duncan Hollow Trail skirts the John Muir Trail; you'll see a high bridge just to the right for hikers to cross the creek. On the other side, you'll reach a junction with the Laurel Fork Creek Trail coinciding with the Fork Ridge Trail to the left. You can use the North Bandy Creek/Katie/Jacks Ridge Loop, the Black House Branch Trail, the Fork Ridge Trail, and the Duncan Hollow Trail to make a loop of 14.6 miles from the Bandy Creek Equestrian Trailhead.

Turn right at this junction, and you'll join the John Muir Trail; the JMT and Duncan Hollow Trail then coincide until the Duncan Hollow Trail soon turns off left while the John Muir Trail stays straight. At 5.6 miles the Duncan Hollow Trail fords Station Camp Creek and continues on to connect with the Station Camp Creek Trail at 5.7 miles. Horse and bike riders can use the North Bandy Creek/Katie/Jacks Ridge Loop, the Black House Branch Trail, the Charit Creek Lodge Trail, the Station Camp Creek Trail, and the Duncan Hollow Trail to make a loop of 16.0 miles from the Bandy Creek Equestrian Trailhead.

⑪ ⑪ Duncan Hollow Loop 🚲

5.0 miles
Moderate
Elevation change: 200 ft.
Cautions: Mudholes, steep descents and ascents
Connections: John Litton Farm Loop 🏃,
Duncan Hollow Trail ∩, Katie Trail ∩, By-Pass Trail ∩

Attractions: This short loop offers a good introduction to mountain biking.

Trailhead: Follow the directions in Trail #3 and park at the swimming pool in the campground. Hikers may use bike trails, but horses are not allowed here except on the Duncan Hollow and By-Pass Roads. Bike trails are blazed for one-way use.

Description: From the pool parking area, head down the graveled Duncan Hollow Road past the John Litton Farm Loop Trailhead on the right. At 0.3 mile the Katie Trail joins the road from the left. North from this junction the road is the Duncan Hollow Trail for horses and is also open to vehicle use.

At 0.9 mile you'll pass under powerlines and reach a right fork headed toward the John Litton Farm; the road is part of the John Litton Farm Loop. The bike loop bears left off the road here, but just stay with the road because the trail soon reconnects. At 1.2 miles the bike trail turns left on By-Pass Road. You'll pass an old road on the right that will be your return route. Stay with the main road left at the trace of an old road to the right at 1.8 miles.

At 1.9 miles the bike trail leaves the road straight ahead as the road curves left. Veer left at another old road right. At 2.3 miles, you'll turn right and descend to ford a small creek. Ascending, you'll encounter an old road and turn right. At 2.7 miles, the trail curves left and descends. You'll then ascend to the top of a hill and turn right on an old road. The trail reconnects with By-Pass Road at 3.6 miles. Turn left to return to Duncan Hollow Road and ride back to the parking area at 5.0 miles.

Mountain Bikers

⅟2 Collier Ridge Loop 🚲

7.3 miles
Moderate
Elevation change: 200 ft.
Cautions: Stream crossings
Connections: Bandy Creek Campground Loop 🚶, North
Bandy Creek Trail ⋂, Oscar Blevins Farm Loop 🚶, West
Entrance Trail 🚶

Attractions: This more difficult loop provides more opportunity for practicing mountain biking skills.

Trailhead: Follow the directions in Trail #1 to the Bandy Creek Trailhead.

Description: From the parking area, bike back out to Bandy Creek Road and turn left. The Bandy Creek Campground Loop crosses the road where it changes to gravel, and at 0.1 mile, the North Bandy Creek Trail for horses crosses the road. You'll pass the Lora Blevins House and Katie Blevins Cemetery at 0.6 mile, and then at 0.8 mile you'll pass a Scott State Forest sign and turn left off the road onto a graveled path. At 0.9 mile you'll cross the Oscar Blevins Farm Loop hiking trail.

The bike trail fords the north branch of Bandy Creek at 1.1 miles. At 1.2 miles the Oscar Blevins Loop joins on the right; the hiking trail and bike trail now coincide on an old roadbed. Soon after, stay left at a fork, which is the junction with the loop part of the bike trail; you'll return on the right fork.

At 1.5 miles, you'll cross King Branch. You'll then ride through the old Billie Blevins farmsite and at 1.7 miles continue straight as the Oscar Blevins Loop turns left off the old roadway. The West Entrance Trail crosses the bike trail at 1.9 miles. You'll then cross the south branch of Bandy Creek at 2.0 miles and then a small creek. Stay right at 2.2 miles. You'll ascend, sometimes on bare rock to emerge onto TN297 at 2.8 miles; turn right on the highway. Watch for a turn back into the woods at 4.2 miles.

At this writing, a connecting trail that will take the loop off the highway is under construction and should be ready in 1995. The trail will begin on your right about 80 yards before you reach TN297. The trail will parallel the highway to the west, dipping through hollows and crossing old roadways and emerging in the clearing along the highway where, at this writing, you turn off to pick up the trail into the woods again. Because of the winding nature of the trail, the new section will add about a half mile to your ride.

Whichever way you arrive at the clearing, following the highway or riding the new section, you'll then head north on the bike trail. At 4.3 miles, turn right on an old road that is also the West Entrance Trail. The bike trail turns left off the road at 4.6 miles while the hiking trail stays with the road. The bike trail becomes mostly a single track winding through the woods.

You'll descend to close the loop at 6.1 miles. Bear left to recross the north branch of Bandy Creek and return to the West Bandy Creek Road at 6.5 miles. Turn right to return to the Bandy Creek Trailhead parking at 7.3 miles.

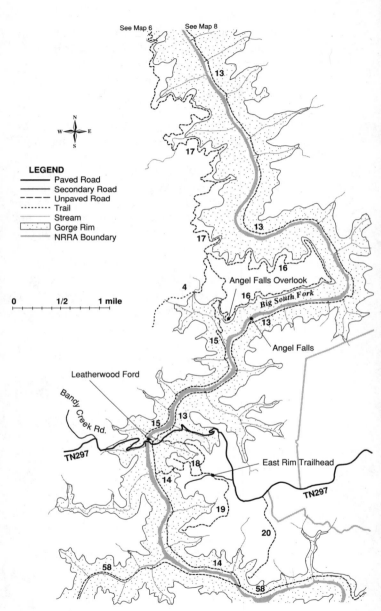

See Map 6
See Map 8

LEGEND
Paved Road
Secondary Road
Unpaved Road
Trail
Stream
Gorge Rim
NRRA Boundary

0   1/2   1 mile

13
17
13
17
16
4
16   Angel Falls Overlook
15   *Big South Fork*
13
Angel Falls

Leatherwood Ford
Bandy Creek Rd.
15   13
TN297
18
14   East Rim Trailhead
19   TN297
20
58
14
58

Map 4. Leatherwood Ford and East Rim
44

1③ Angel Falls Trail 👣
River Trail East ∩

8.1 miles one-way
(Angel Falls 2.0 miles one-way)
Easy to Angel Falls, then moderate
Elevation change: 100 ft.
Cautions: Can get muddy and overgrown beyond Angel Falls
Connections: John Muir Trail 👣, Smith Ridge Trail ∩,
Big Island Loop ∩

Attractions: Along this river trail featuring rock bluffs and a view of Angel Falls, you'll enjoy wildflowers in the spring.

Trailhead: On TN297, from the junction of Bandy Creek Road, head east to descend into the river gorge and cross the river over the bridge at Leatherwood Ford and turn left into the river access on the east side of the river; you'll find restrooms and a large parking area. If you're coming from the east on TN297, you'll enter the park and descend into the river gorge to Leatherwood Ford at 2.2 miles from the east entrance.

Description: The John Muir Trail comes from the south to cross the river on the old wooden Leatherwood Ford Bridge, which was the only way to cross the river before the new high bridge was built and the road paved. To begin the Angel Falls Trail, walk to the far north end of the parking area and follow the old road headed upstream, paralleling the river.

You'll stroll through the shade of hemlocks, rhododendron, and mixed hardwood. Numbered posts corresponding to a brochure available at the information gazebo in the parking area identify the trees; the posts begin along the sidewalk north of the gazebo. In spring columbine, trillium, geranium, and more also line the trail. At 0.1 mile you'll cross a small stream on a footbridge. Then at 0.8 mile, the trail crosses Anderson Branch on another bridge. The reclaimed Anderson coal mine lies off to the right.

The trail passes a rock bluff on your right at 1.2 miles where you'll have a good view of the river. At 1.3 miles you'll rockhop a small stream. Along the way, watch for a rock bluff on the right that contains a coal seam you can reach up and touch.

At 1.8 miles, a side path leading to the river and rejoining the main trail is the access for the portage around Angel Falls. At 2.0 miles you'll reach a trail junction with Angel Falls to the left; the old road continues on toward Station Camp Crossing to the right. Take the left fork to a wooden deck overlooking Angel Falls, a huge rapids formed by boulders standing in the river. The rapids are all that's left of a low waterfall dynamited in the 1950s, probably by fishermen hoping to improve navigation on the river. There was little improvement. Although the falls is no longer a waterfall, it's still an impressive sight, a churning sluice of water that rushes downstream.

This side trail is the portage for boats to reenter the river downstream from the rapids. If you follow it down and explore along the river, you must use caution. If you slip on the rocks and fall in the water, the swift current will sling you against boulders and perhaps trap you underwater. A hiker drowned here in 1988.

At the junction where you go down to Angel Falls, bear right uphill to continue north on the River Trail East. You'll ascend to a gate at 2.1 miles; those on horses and mountain bikes coming from the other direction must leave horses and bikes here and walk down to Angel Falls.

The trail continues paralleling the river to the north, sometimes ascending over low ridges. At 3.2 miles the trail curves right to cross Bill Branch. The trail then ascends to the John Smith Place at 3.3 miles, which was Smith's homesite and once the location of a mining operation. An old road that turns up to the right will eventually be part of the proposed Smith Ridge Trail that fords the river from the west and from here heads up to TN297 northeast of the Black Oak Church; at this writing the route is unblazed and not maintained.

Beyond the John Smith Place, the trail can be muddy and in summer, overgrown, but at a time we hiked the trail in late summer, the path was dry and had been recently cleared.

The trail descends from the John Smith Place and soon crosses a culvert that drains a hollow on the right with huge boulders. You'll then gently ascend through a grassy area to the site of an old mine on the right at 3.4 miles. The trail ascends above the mine area. You'll cross a small stream turned rust-colored with oxides it has picked up while draining the mine area.

You'll descend to river level at 3.9 miles where you'll walk over river rock in the floodplain. You'll have to rockhop Rough Shoals Branch that flows into the river. At 4.1 miles notice a chute resting atop a small rock overhang on the right, left from mining operations up the slope. At 4.2 miles you'll step over a wet-weather stream that has a trickle of a waterfall dropping off a rock wall to your right; in summer you'll see white wood aster.

The trail descends a sandy slope to a footbridge crossing of a stream near the river at 4.3 miles. The trail soon curves right up a hollow to cross a small stream flowing out of boulders with a rock overhang. Watch for tall stands of yellow coneflowers and sunflowers in late summer.

At 4.8 miles you'll pass a small pond hidden in the trees on the right and then hop on large stepping stones to avoid a wet area. At another pond, frogs leap into the water in summer and red cardinal flowers stand at the water's edge. The trail soon crosses a small stream draining a nearby mine area.

The trail passes over a knoll. Watch for stands of cane and reed. At 5.8 miles the trail drops to cross a wet-weather stream and soon after descends with waterbars to cross Blevins Branch; when we were last there a collapsed bridge marked the crossing, but the trail will be relocated above this area.

At 6.2 miles, the trail drops to cross Mill Creek; both banks of the stream can be muddy. The trail then curves back to the left and passes a bridge that once spanned the creek crossing but was washed to this location by floodwaters. The trail curves right at 6.4 miles to go up another hollow to drop down stone steps to a creek crossing. Notice large beech trees in the area.

You'll cross several small streams before passing through the parking area at Station Camp Crossing at 8.1 miles. You'll connect with the Station Camp Road; the Big Island Loop turns off the road to the right soon after the road crosses Slavens Branch. At low water, you can also ford the river to the other side to connect with the Station Camp Creek Trail and the John Muir Trail. Ford only at low water.

¹4 O&W Bridge 🚶🚶

2.3 miles one-way
Moderate
Elevation change: 100 ft.
Cautions: Creek crossings, short steep ascent
Connections: Angel Falls 🚶🚶/River Trail East ∩, John Muir
Trail 🚶🚶, Leatherwood Ford Loop 🚶🚶

Attractions: Enjoy river and bluff views along this trail to the O&W Railroad Bridge. Wildflowers are plentiful in the spring.

Trailhead: Follow the directions in Trail #13 to the Leatherwood Ford River Access. The Angel Falls Trail heads to the north while the John Muir Trail crosses the old Leatherwood Ford Bridge to head north on the other side of the river.

Description: To head toward the O&W Bridge, walk south under the TN297 bridge to a trail junction. If you climb the rock steps on your left to the highway above, you'd be on the Leatherwood Ford Loop. Continue straight into the woods headed south; this is also the John Muir Trail, blazed with a blue silhouette of John Muir.

With the river on your right, you'll cross a wooden bridge and meander through a fern and wildflower gathering and boulder displays. This part of the trail is graveled and smooth and has occasional benches to make it universally accessible. Watch for platforms and stairs off to the right that let you play among boulders at the river's edge. At 0.3 mile, you'll leave the universally accessible portion of the trail and walk on an old roadbed that parallels the river. You'll drop through a drainage that leads right to the river at a large pool across from the mouth of Bandy Creek on the river's west side.

This section of the John Muir Trail is also part of the Leatherwood Ford Loop. At 0.5 mile you'll encounter a junction, where the loop turns left up the steep slope toward the East Rim Trailhead. Continue straight ahead to stay on the John Muir Trail. You'll cross a small creek, dry at times, and then follow the trail down right as the old road continues left uphill. At 0.8 mile you'll begin a climb up the slope on rock steps and switch-backs.

At 1.0 mile, the trail rejoins an old road and descends to once more reach a level area paralleling the river. Where the river curves to the left, you can perhaps see through the trees across to the confluence of North White Oak Creek. You'll stay with the road now, crossing occasional wet-weather streams, sometimes on footbridges, until at 2.1 miles you'll have your first view of the O&W Bridge and pass huge boulders to the left of the trail. As you near the bridge, you'll encounter a house-sized boulder that fell from the rim and landed in the roadway. The trail turns down right to go around the boulder and arrives at the O&W railbed and the bridge over the Big South Fork at 2.3 miles

The Oneida and Western Railroad Bridge was a link in the now-abandoned O&W Railroad that connected Oneida with Jamestown to the west, a rail line of 37 miles. The O&W Bridge was erected in 1915 and abandoned in 1954; the train rails were pulled up and sold as scrap when the trains stopped operating. The bridge has a Whipple Truss design that was used between 1847 and 1900. This 200-foot bridge was once on another railroad but was brought here and adapted for use by the O&W. Very few Whipple Truss bridges survive today.

The John Muir Trail currently ends at the O&W Bridge, but plans call for the trail to cross the bridge and then to continue south on the west side of the river by first climbing Hurricane Ridge and eventually following the Clear Fork River all the way to the southern boundary of the park at Peters Bridge, which would add about 23 miles to the trail. A first section is expected to be completed in 1995.

From the bridge, enjoy the view of rock bluffs overhead; below, you'll see rapids stretching upstream before the river fades around the bend. A wooden stairway provides access to the river's edge on the upstream side of the bridge. Unless you have a shuttle to pick you up here, retrace your walk back to Leatherwood Ford.

O&W Bridge
50

15 Angel Falls Overlook 🚶🚶

3.0 miles one-way
Moderate
Elevation gain: 400 ft.
Cautions: Stream crossings, steep ascent, boulder passages,
narrow ledge crossing, ladder
Connections: Angel Falls 🚶🚶/River Trail East ∩, Grand Gap
Loop 🚶🚶, John Muir Trail 🚶🚶

Attractions: This trail takes you along the river, past rushing streams, through boulder passages, and atop the plateau for one of the best views of the Big South Fork Gorge. Wildflowers are plentiful in spring along the river.

Trailhead: Follow the directions in Trail #13 to the Leatherwood Ford River Access where the Angel Falls Trail heads to the north and the John Muir Trail heads south toward the O&W Bridge.

Description: To get to Angel Falls Overlook, you must hike the John Muir Trail north on the other side of the river. Walk across the old Leatherwood Ford Bridge and climb the stairs into the woods. Then turn right towards Fall Branch. If there has been a recent rain, the old bridge may be underwater; in that case you'll have to walk across the highway bridge to get across the river and then make your way down to pick up the trail.

With rock bluffs on your left laced with laurel blossoms in May and the river drifting below on your right, you will encounter several side streams, cascades, and bridges as you meander through a hemlock and mixed-hardwood forest. This part of the trail is a wonderland of wildflowers in spring. You'll see crested dwarf iris, bluets, cinquefoil, penstemon, fire pink, geranium, purple phacelia, foamflower, may apple, marsh blue violets, trillium, bloodroot, dwarf dandelion, and more. If you are just out for a stroll, this first part of the trail is an easy walk and a good one in spring.

At 1.8 miles you'll begin paralleling Fall Branch upstream from where it joins the Big South Fork. At 2.0 miles the trail crosses a curved bridge over Fall Branch, which roars and rushes through boulders as it hurries to the river. On the other side, you'll walk downstream with a rock bluff on your left and the stream on your right before you make a switchback up to the left.

The trail is then mostly a continuous climb with switchbacks, stone steps, and boulder passages. The trail runs into a large boulder; bear left. You'll then reach the rim rock, bear left again. The trail then levels off for a time with the rock bluff on your right and the valley of Fall Branch on your left. The trail passes under a rock overhang and crosses a wet-weather stream.

At 2.6 miles, you'll switchback onto a rock shelf as the trail leads into a small gorge created by the stream you just crossed. There's a cable to hang onto. Notice the iron deposits in the rock face along the ledge. Climb the ladder and follow the trail as it ascends through a hemlock and rhododendron cove sandwiched between gorge walls. Toward the upper end you'll pass large beech trees.

When you arrive at the top at 2.8 miles, the trail connects with the Grand Gap Loop. Turn right to get to the Angel Falls Overlook for a grand view of the river in another 0.2 mile. You must continue along the Grand Gap Loop a few paces past the first overlook to actually get a view of Angel Falls below. But the first overlook is the best with the river sweeping by vertical rock walls, perhaps the best view in the park and one of the best on the entire Cumberland Plateau.

Retracing your steps, you'll have a total hike of 6 miles.

Angel Falls Overlook

16 Grand Gap Loop 𝕩𝕩

6.8 miles
(Grand Gap Overlook 1.0 mile one-way)
Easy
Mostly level
Cautions: High bluffs
Connections: John Muir Trail 𝕩𝕩, Fall Branch Trail 𝕩𝕩

Attractions: This loop offers spectacular views of the Big South Fork and Angel Falls.

Trailhead: Follow the directions in Trail #13 to the Leatherwood Ford River Access and walk Trail #15 2.8 miles to the Grand Gap Loop.

Description: Once you get to the Grand Gap Loop, you can turn right or left to hike the loop. To the left is the continuation of the John Muir Trail. Turn right to get to Angel Falls Overlook. The trail continues past the main overlook, paralleling the gorge rim past other views where you can see Angel Falls far below.

The rest of the trail for most of the loop periodically swings away from the gorge edge then returns, remaining relatively level with only a few ups and downs. You'll be passing through the typical pine and mixed hardwood Uplands Forest of the plateau-top. In spring, you'll see occasional yellow stargrass and violet wood sorrel.

After the first overlooks, the trail swings away from the bluff edge. At 0.4 mile, you'll follow a rock bluff on the left and come to a moss-covered arch, about 8 feet high and 50 feet long. Soon after, the trail passes by a rock overhang.

At 1.0 mile, watch for the trail to make a sharp switchback right. The trail appears to go straight because most people have missed the turn and created a path straight ahead. If you miss it too, you'll find the trail just disappears; retrace your steps, and you'll see the trail headed downhill. You'll switchback down to the bluff edge, where a short path takes you to a narrow promontory that thrusts you out for a wide-angle view of Angel Falls upstream. This Grand Gap Overlook is well worth the walk.

You'll soon turn away from the gorge. At 1.4 miles the trail crosses a little footbridge over a seep that comes from under a rock overhang. Later, the trail enters a hemlock woods at 1.9 miles and joins an old roadbed at 2.1 miles at Grand Gap.

Turn right on the roadbed, and then in a few yards the trail turns left off the road. You'll pass another rock overhang at 2.2 miles and then top out on a bluff at 2.4 miles. The trail then switchbacks left and climbs up and over a small ridge.

At 3.1 miles the trail again joins an old roadbed. Turn right, and in a few yards the trail turns left away from the road. At 3.7 miles the trail comes to a bluff overlooking a tributary gorge of the Big South Fork. Massive stone walls stand across the way. The trail soon rejoins the old roadbed; then it swings right from the road to an overlook where this side gorge joins the river gorge.

The trail then rejoins the road, ascends slightly, crosses another old roadbed at 4.0 miles, and then again at 4.4 miles. At 5.2 miles the trail loops around an open area that was once the homesite of Alfred and Elva Smith. Alfred was a logger for the Stearns Coal and Lumber Company. When the lumbering operations were discontinued in the 1940s, the Smiths left their plateau retreat, leaving behind their son Archie, who was only four months old when he died of pneumonia in 1932. His grave is at 6.1 miles along the trail.

Before that, you'll reach a junction at 5.5 miles with the John Muir Trail to the right, headed north. Turn left on the John Muir Trail to complete the Grand Gap Loop. You'll cross an old road at 5.6 miles and reach a junction with the Fall Branch Trail to the right that leads 1.9 miles to the John Litton Farm Loop.

Continuing on past the grave of Archie Smith, you'll reach the valley of Fall Branch at 6.6 miles on the right. You'll have a broad sandstone bluff from which to view where Fall Branch joins the Big South Fork at 6.7 miles. You'll then parallel on the right the small cove that contains the John Muir Trail down to Leatherwood Ford and complete the loop at 6.8 miles. The total round-trip hiking distance from Leatherwood Ford is 12.4 miles.

17 John Muir Trail 🚶🚶

42 miles one-way
Moderate
Elevation change: 500 ft.
Cautions: Steep ascents and descents, creek fords, bluff
dropoffs
Connections: Grand Gap Loop 🚶🚶, Fall Branch Trail 🚶🚶,
Duncan Hollow Trail ∩, Laurel Fork Creek Trail 🚶🚶, Station
Camp Creek Trail ∩, Parch Corn Trail ∩, Big Branch Trail ∩,
Watson Cemetery Trail ∩, Maude's Crack Overlook Loop 🚶🚶,
No Business Trail ∩, Dry Branch Trail 🚶🚶, Stoopin Oak
Trail ∩, Rock Creek Loop 🚶🚶, Sheltowee Trace 🚶🚶,
Rock Creek Trail 🚶🚶, Hidden Passage Trail 🚶🚶

Attractions: Maybe the best four- or five-day backpack in the
Southeast, the John Muir Trail leads by gorge overlooks, tumbling streams, pioneer homesites, rock walls and buttes. This national historic trail commemorates the 1867 journey through this
plateau country by the noted conservationist and founder of the
Sierra Club. Although Muir became famous wandering the Sierras
in California, the Cumberlands were the first mountains he explored. The trail is blazed by a blue silhouette of John Muir.

Trailhead: The easiest southern access for the John Muir Trail
is at Leatherwood Ford River Access on TN297; follow the directions in Trail #13. The JMT actually extends south from
Leatherwood Ford 2.3 miles to the O&W Bridge and will eventually extend farther south to Peters Bridge at the southern boundary of the park. Our mileages begin at Leatherwood Ford.

Description: Walk across the old low-water bridge to the west
side of the river and turn right, downstream. At 2.0 miles, you'll
cross a bridge over Fall Branch, the last reliable source of water
for the next section of trail, and ascend to the top of the plateau
to the Grand Gap Loop at 2.8 miles. (See Trail #15 for details.)
　　Turn left at the junction to continue the JMT. You'll pass an
overlook of the Fall Branch Gorge at 2.9 miles. The trail passes

the grave of Archie Smith at 3.5 miles and reaches a junction with the Fall Branch Trail to the left at 4.0 miles. It's 0.1 mile down the trail to a tributary of Fall Branch that usually has water. Continuing straight, you'll cross a dirt road and reach a junction at 4.1 miles where the Grand Gap Loop comes in from the right and the JMT continues left, headed north. You, of course, can hike the Grand Gap Loop to this point (see Trail #16).

The trail now wends through the woods, paralleling the rim, with an occasional gorge view. At 4.7 miles, cross an old road. At 4.8 miles, watch for a left turn in the trail; you'll soon cross bare rock with reindeer moss and pines in pockets of thin soil.

Watch for a right turn uphill at 5.1 miles. The trail crosses a small creek at 5.8 miles where you might find water; to the left you'll see a pouroff where water coming out of the bluffs drops to the creekbed. At 6.2 miles, cross an old roadway and then watch for a turn left at 6.3 miles.

The trail at 6.6 miles crosses a drainage on a footbridge that was broken down when we were last there. You'll cross another footbridge, and then at 7.0 miles a short stairway takes you down a low bluff. Turn left and follow the JMT out along the bluff to a good view of the sandstone rim of the river gorge.

At 7.6 miles, the trail makes a right turn to a junction; the main trail turns left and a side path straight leads to a gorge overlook on a point. You'll reach another junction at 8.2 miles where the main trail turns left and a side trail straight leads out to an overlook where a side cove on the left joins the river gorge. The JMT now heads up this tributary cove to descend through a couple of switchbacks and cross a footbridge over a side drainage and then reach a bridge over the main tributary creek at 10.3 miles. This is the only reliable source of water on the 13-mile stretch from Fall Branch to Laurel Fork. You'll find some areas for camping just upstream.

The trail now heads up the other side of the cove back toward the river. You'll then bear left to parallel the river and eventually bear left up Duncan Hollow. You'll penetrate deep into the hollow and cross a ridge. At 12.9 miles, the trail crosses an old road. You'll cross a saddle and then ascend to join an old road at 13.2 miles. Follow the road to the right. At 13.6 miles, the trail turns off left and descends toward Station Camp Creek.

The trail crosses a footbridge over a small drainage and descends into a beech cove. You'll cross another footbridge and circle the point of a ridge and switchback right down to face a massive block of stone; turn left down stone steps to get around the obstruction. The trail then makes a series of switchbacks to complete the descent. At 14.8 miles the trail passes above the confluence of Laurel Fork and Station Camp Creek and follows Laurel Fork upstream. You'll drop into the overgrown floodplain where the Duncan Hollow Trail comes down to ford the creek; you'll find a high bridge over Laurel Fork at 15.0 miles.

On the other side, the Laurel Fork Creek Trail leads to the left. Turn right to stay with the JMT. At another junction; the Duncan Hollow Trail turns to the left. The JMT bears right along an old road, but soon turns left to cross Station Camp Creek on a bridge at 15.1 miles. After crossing the bridge, the JMT bears right through an overgrown area to rejoin the old road, which has forded the creek. Turn left. At 15.4 miles, the trail turns left off the road, which continues on toward the Station Camp River Crossing. The JMT passes through an overgrown area with foundations and building debris. A subsistence farming community once thrived on Station Camp Creek. The community had a grocery store, post office, school, and survived into the early 1960s in the face of a dwindling population.

At 15.5 miles, you'll reach a junction with the Station Camp Creek Trail. Charit Creek Lodge lies several miles to the left; 0.2 mile down to the right you can reach the Station Camp River Crossing. To stay on the JMT, keep straight up an old road, which is also the Parch Corn Trail. At 15.6 miles, the JMT bears left, while the horse trail continues along the road.

The trail climbs above the road to traverse a broad shelf until at 16.0 miles you'll cross a bridge over a drainage. Soon after, the JMT rejoins the road. At 16.4 miles, as the road nears Parch Corn Creek, the trail bears left through an overgrown area. You'll cross a bridge over a side drainage and reach a long bridge over Parch Corn Creek at 16.6 miles.

On the other side of the bridge, you'll encounter the old Parch Corn Road, which is now the Parch Corn Trail. You can turn left for 0.2 mile to reach the John Litton Cabin built in 1881; do not camp in the cabin or the cabin's yard. The JMT turns right

Bridge over Laurel Fork

on Parch Corn Road from the bridge crossing and then leaves the road to the left. The road continues on down to connect with the road/horse trail along the river after it has forded Parch Corn Creek. As the JMT continues north it weaves on and off the old river road, which is now the Big Branch Trail.

At 16.9 miles, the trail swings away from the road to cross a bridge over Harvey Branch. You'll cross two more bridges over smaller streams. Watch for rock foundations and piles of stone from cleared fields, remnants of settlements along the road that connected the main communities at Parch Corn and No Business Creeks. At 18.1 miles, the Watson Cemetery Trail leading down from Terry Cemetery Road crosses the JMT to connect with the Big Branch Trail. At 18.3 miles, the JMT curves left up a side road toward a bridge over Big Branch. When we were last there, the bridge had been washed a few yards downstream; so we forded the creek on the road.

The JMT continues to parallel the road until at 18.5 miles it turns uphill to the left; if you have been walking the road instead of the trail, you'll need to watch for this junction up the slope to your left. The old road continues north another mile to the mouth of No Business Creek.

Turn left uphill to continue on the JMT. You'll soon swing right up Big Branch Hollow on an old roadway, sometimes steeply. At 19.2 miles, the trail bears right off the road. You'll continue up to cross another road. The trail switchbacks right and left, crisscrossing this old roadway. If leaves are off the trees, you'll see two huge stone pillars standing on the ridge up to your right.

The trail makes a switchback right with a tall sandstone bluff standing ahead. At 19.4 miles, the trail tops the ridge where a path coming in from the left is the unofficial Maude's Crack Overlook Loop. The pillars you saw from below stand to the right.

The JMT turns back left over the ridge and circles the rock bluff with some of the most intricate rockwork we've seen. The trail crosses a ridge below the point of the bluff and circles left to cross a saddle between the main bluff and a sandstone knob.

At 19.7 miles, the JMT switchbacks right to begin a descent toward No Business Creek. Just at the turn, you'll see a passageway to the left where the Maude's Crack Overlook Loop turns off to head up to Maude's Crack. On the JMT, you'll descend into a valley of sandstone buttes, several to the left while you pass below Burke Knob to the right.

After many switchbacks, you'll bottom out at 20.5 miles and turn left to cross two footbridges over Betty Branch. Then turn right to reach a long bridge over No Business Creek; when we were last there the bridge was a bit lopsided; take care. On the other side of the creek, good camping spots lie to the right.

The trail bears left to enter the former community of No Business and pass the foundations for the old boarding house; the pillars are solid sandstone slabs. The community adopted the creek's name, which is attributed to the wife of an early settler who said they had no business being there. The community had two stores, a school, a post office and survived into the 1960s.

The trail passes through a grassy area and up to a junction with an old road at 20.7 miles. This road is a multiple-use trail— the No Business Trail for horses, and the Dry Branch Trail to the right and the JMT to the left for hikers.

Hiking left along the road, you'll parallel No Business Creek upstream. Watch for foundations and the remains of fences. At 21.4 miles, an old road turns down to ford the creek; you'll see foundations across the way. At 21.5 miles, watch for the shell of an old truck where a side stream crosses under slabs of rock in the road and tumbled-down log barns rest in the overgrown field to the left. Soon after, you'll pass the Stoopin Oak Trail headed up the slope to the right. At 21.6 miles, the JMT fords Tacket Creek, the last reliable source of water for the next leg. Then at 21.9 miles, the JMT turns right off the old road; the No Business Trail continues on to connect with the Longfield Branch Trail.

Turning right, you'll begin a long climb to the top of the plateau. The trail switchbacks right and left and then hits an old roadway at 22.1 miles where you'll turn right. But then watch for a turn left off the road at 22.2 miles; the turn is easy to miss. You'll make several more switchbacks to climb a ladder up a low bluff and walk up stone steps to a left turn. After a couple more switchbacks, the trail runs into a slope of bare stone at 23.0 miles. Scramble up the stone and watch for the trail turning right. You'll finally reach the top at 23.1 miles. The trail then swings left to the bare rock of the John Muir Overlook at 23.2 miles, a

Foundations of the Boarding House

panoramic view of the No Business Creek Gorge.

From the overlook, head right along the bluff. The trail drops to cross a narrow ridge separating No Business Creek Gorge from Tacket Creek Gorge. At 23.4 miles, you'll turn left on an old road. Then at 23.8 miles, the trail turns left off the road just before you reach posts blocking vehicle access from the other direction, which is the short way in to the John Muir Overlook.

The next section of trail is uneventful. You'll cross old roads at first and later a number of footbridges over small streams. At 28.6 miles, you must bear right through a downfall, if it has not been cleared, to reach a short ladder up a low bluff. At 30.7 miles, you'll ascend to cross Divide Road. The trail then descends with switchbacks to cross Massey Branch on a bridge and connect with the Rock Creek Loop at 31.2 miles.

The JMT now follows the Rock Creek Loop to the right (see Trail #44). At 32.4 miles, you'll reach a junction with the Sheltowee Trace and then all three trails coincide as the path turns left and follows Rock Creek upstream. At 35.8 miles, you'll reach a junction with the Rock Creek Loop turning up left and the JMT/Sheltowee Trace turning down right to ford Rock Creek. On the other side, turn left upstream to cross into Pickett State Forest. A concrete piling perched on a rock on the other side of the creek once supported a railroad bridge.

You'll then connect with the Rock Creek Trail at 36.0 miles. At the junction, you have the option of continuing straight on the Rock Creek Trail, passing the junction with the Tunnel Trail and fording the creek three times to reach TN154 at 37.9 miles (see Trail #84). From there, if you want to walk farther, walk to the right on the highway to cross the bridge over Rock Creek and turn left back into the woods. In the next few miles, you'll make 27 fords and 2 bridge crossings of Rock Creek. At 42.9 miles, you'll reach Boundary Road and the end of the JMT.

The other option at the junction with the Rock Creek Trail is to turn left rather than stay straight along the creek. You'll ford to the other side and make a steep ascent out of the gorge. At 37.5 miles you'll connect with the Hidden Passage Trail Loop. Turn left. You'll pass by Thompson Overlook and continue on to emerge at the trailhead for the Hidden Passage Trail on TN154 at 42.4 miles (see Trail #83).

⅂⑧ Leatherwood Ford Loop 🚶🚶

3.6 miles
Moderate
Elevation change: 550 ft.
Cautions: Short section along highway
Connections: Sunset Overlook Trail 🚶🚶, John Muir Trail 🚶🚶

Attractions: The upper part of the loop offers scenic views and blooming laurel in mid-May; in early spring, you'll walk through gatherings of wildflowers on the lower elevations and along the river.

Trailhead: Head up the east side of the river gorge from Leatherwood Ford on TN297, and at 1.6 miles turn right on the paved road across from the park headquarters where a sign directs you to the East Rim Overlook. If you're entering the park from the east on TN297, you'll encounter the turn on your left at 0.6 mile from the park's east entrance sign. At 0.3 mile along the road to the East Rim Overlook, park on the right at the East Rim Trailhead. You'll see the old dirt Leatherwood Ford Road leading into the clearing. On the other side of the paved road, the Sunset Overlook Trail heads south.

Description: On the trailhead side of the road, walk to the left, paralleling the road, until you enter the woods and the trail becomes more obvious. In 0.2 mile you'll reach the loop part of the trail. Turn left for the best approach.

You'll pass through a low area that has water in wet seasons, join an old road for a short distance, and then drop among rocks to a side trail at 0.6 mile; the path leads to the right 0.1 mile to an overlook of the river with the bridge at Leatherwood Ford.

Back on the main trail, you'll descend more obviously, following a small stream and passing below rock bluffs to eventually rockhop the stream. The trail works through several switchbacks before it reaches the river at 1.6 miles. This section of the trail wanders through wildflowers in spring—foamflower, pen-

Leatherwood Ford Overlook

stemon, geranium, columbine, solomon's seal, phlox, cinque-foil, crested dwarf iris, blood root, fire pink, may apple, dwarf dandelion, and more.

At the river, the trail joins the John Muir Trail. You can turn left here to reach the old O&W Railroad Bridge in 1.8 miles. To continue the loop, turn right on the JMT. The trail parallels the river and eventually becomes a graveled path leading to Leatherwood Ford at 2.1 miles.

Next to the TN297 bridge, before going under, turn right and go up the rock steps beside the bridge. After topping out on the highway, walk up the road, which passes over a creek, to a right turn into the woods.

The trail climbs steeply from the highway through a number of switchbacks. You'll see an old road off to the right and then cross it at 2.6 miles. This is the old Leatherwood Ford wagon road that once led down the bluff to the river ford and that you saw at the trailhead; the old road was used as the route for the water line running to the restrooms at the river, so you'll see some scars left from the digging and occasional metal plates that cover access to the water line, like here where the trail meets the road. At 2.7 miles the trail approaches the creek that you crossed on the road as it cascades among boulders on its way down the slope, here making a small waterfall in a cove of rhododendron and hemlock. The trail switches left and then passes through more switchbacks to cross the old road again at 2.9 miles. The trail then swings right to follow the road up the ridge.

Once you reach the top of the gorge, you'll turn right off the road to follow the border between field and forest until you cross a footbridge and pass over the earthen dam for an old farm pond on your left at 3.3 miles. A short hike through the woods returns you to the beginning of the loop at 3.4 miles; turn left to return to the trailhead at 3.6 miles.

1⑨ Sunset Overlook Trail 🚶🚶

1.3 miles one-way
Easy
Level
Cautions: High cliffs
Connections: Leatherwood Ford Loop 🚶🚶

Attractions: This trail leads to an overlook with a panoramic view of the river gorge and Leatherwood Ford.

Trailhead: Follow the directions in Trail #18 to the East Rim Trailhead.

Description: Cross the road from trailhead parking and take the trail into the woods. You'll swing left to emerge on a gravel road at 0.1 mile that leads off the paved road up to a small building at a shooting range for law enforcement officers. Cross the road and pass by a pond on the left. This path was once a nature trail; you may still see some old posts with interpretive numbers.

You'll parallel a small creek on the left and then turn to cross the creek on a bridge at 0.3 mile. The trail skirts the back of a maintenance and office area that you'll see through the trees to the left. You'll then curve right to cross an earthen dam creating another pond at 0.4 mile; a footbridge takes you over the spill-way. You'll then join an old roadway and turn to the right.

At 0.6 mile, the trail turns right off the road. But then at 0.7 mile, the trail rejoins the road where you'll turn right. You'll pass the trace of old roads to the right and left as you stay with the main roadway. At 1.1 miles the roadway narrows to a path in a small open area with two beech trees standing on the left; this may have been a housesite that the road led to.

Continue on the path out the point of the bluff and descend to the edge of the gorge with switchbacks left and right down to the bare rock of Sunset Overlook with a great view of the river gorge. To the right, you'll see the TN297 bridge at Leatherwood Ford and to the left the North White Oak Creek drainage.

2⓪ O & W Overlook 🚲

1.1 miles one-way
Easy
Elevation loss: 140 ft.
Cautions: Not blazed, mudholes, high cliffs
Connections: None

Attractions: This old road takes you out to a panoramic view of the river gorge and the O & W Bridge. Until developed, this route should only be attempted by experienced outdoors people.

Trailhead: Just inside the park's east entrance on TN297, you'll see a dirt road on the south side of the highway. Park at this entrance so you do not block the road, or pull up the road a few yards to where you'll see a place to park. The road into the overlook can be negotiated only with four-wheel drive.

Description: Head up the old road into the woods. Unless there has been dry weather, you'll soon begin encountering deep mudholes. You'll have some ups and downs and a somewhat steep rutted descent along the way as you walk or bike ride out the ridge. This route has been proposed as part of a multi-use hiking/mountain bike route to be called the "East Rim Trail," which will eventually connect the O&W Overlook with the Sunset Overlook and then use the Sunset Overlook Trail to connect with the road to the East Rim Overlook.

At 0.8 mile, you'll pass an old roadway to the left as the main road curves right. Then at 1.0 mile, you'll reach the end of the road. Walk the footpath that leads straight into the woods down to the edge of the river gorge, where you'll bear right along the rim to then switchback left down to a bare rock overlook at 1.1 miles. You'll see the O & W Bridge down to your left where it spans the river and have a grand view of the river gorge to the right as the Big South Fork heads toward Leatherwood Ford. Be careful exploring along the edge of the bluff, and do not climb on rocks at the edge; it's a long way down.

O&W Overlook

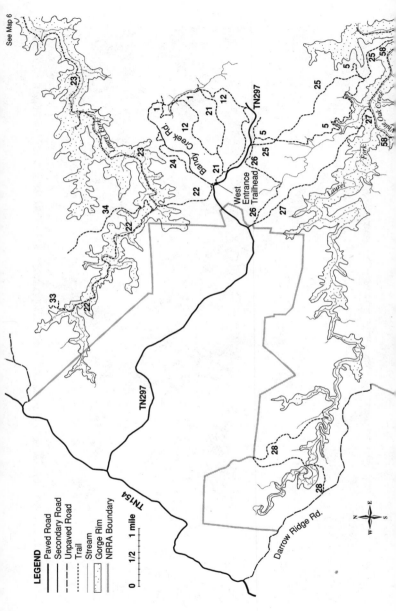

Map 5. West Entrance

70

21 West Entrance Trail 👭

2.4 miles one-way
Easy
Elevation loss: 200 ft.
Cautions: None
Connections: Salt Pine Trail 👭, Collier Ridge Loop 🚲,
Oscar Blevins Farm Loop 👭

Attractions: This easy walk connects the West Entrance Trailhead with the Oscar Blevins Farm Loop.

Trailhead: On the west side of the river, just inside the West Entrance to the BSFNRRA on TN297, turn into parking for the West Entrance Trailhead on the north side of the road. If you're coming from the Visitor Center, the trailhead is 3.9 miles west along TN297 from the Bandy Creek Road turnoff. You can also reach the trailhead from the Visitor Center by continuing on the Bandy Creek Road, which becomes the graveled West Bandy Creek Road and swings around to rejoin TN297 where you'll see the trailhead parking to your left.

Description: At this trailhead, you can also access the Salt Pine Trail to the left, which connects with the Laurel Fork Creek Trail. The West Entrance Trail begins to the right.

At first you'll walk through scrub pine and hardwood as the trail parallels the road to the east. Then at 0.1 mile, you'll curve away from the highway; watch for climbing fern on the right of the trail and a large pine on the left. The trail soon curves back to skirt the highway once more before turning back into the woods.

At 0.4 mile, you'll reach an old road that is now part of the Collier Ridge Loop. Keep straight ahead around a sign that indicates no jeeps, horses, or motorized bikes on this section. The trail follows the old road, except when it veers around mudholes or deep ruts, until at 0.8 mile the bicycle trail forks to the left while the hiking trail continues on the old road to the right; you'll see a faint blaze on a tree ahead. Then at 0.9 mile, the trail turns

71

right off the road and begins dropping.

The trail switchbacks left at 1.0 mile and becomes more closed in by mixed pine and hardwood. You'll see a number of small pine trees. Later you'll find yourself on an old roadbed again. At 1.6 miles you'll reach the south branch of Bandy Creek that wanders through thick laurel. Four footbridges help you across a boggy area where a small stream crosses the trail. At 1.7 miles, you'll enter Scott State Forest.

Watch for trailing arbutus in bloom in spring along the trail. At 2.0 miles you'll pass through a white pine and hemlock grove. Then at 2.2 miles, the trail crosses another old road that is the other side of the Collier Ridge Loop; keep straight.

At 2.4 miles, you'll reach the junction with the Oscar Blevins Farm Loop. To the left on the loop you can walk one mile to the Oscar Blevins Farm, which is now a historic site, and then on to the Bandy Creek Trailhead in another 1.6 miles. Or you can reach the Bandy Creek Trailhead in 1.0 mile by turning right on the loop.

22 Salt Pine/Laurel Fork Creek Trails to the Middle Creek Area 🚶🚶

5.6 miles one-way
Difficult
Elevation change: 420 ft.
Cautions: Many creek crossings impassable in high water,
steep stone steps
Connections: West Entrance Trail 🚶🚶, Laurel Fork Creek Trail
to Station Camp Creek 🚶🚶, Slave Falls Loop 🚶🚶

Attractions: Along these trails into the Middle Creek area, you'll enjoy isolated backcountry while following the Laurel Fork of Station Camp Creek upstream.

Trailhead: Follow the directions in Trail #21 to the West Entrance Trailhead.

Directions: To the right from the parking area, you'll see the West Entrance Trail heading east to the Bandy Creek area. To reach the Middle Creek area, go left, walking west from the parking area and paralleling TN297; this Salt Pine Trail is proposed to become a multi-use path that horses and mountain bikes may also use; check with the rangers at the Visitor Center for when the change is to occur. This trail is also proposed to cross TN297 to the south and connect with the Groom Branch Trail to reach the Cumberland Valley Trailhead.

You'll cross West Bandy Creek Road and continue heading west into the woods. At 0.1 mile the trail crosses an old roadbed at an angle. Soon after this road crossing, you'll reach an old route back to your right; stay straight. Then at 0.2 mile, watch for where the trail curves left back toward the highway; hikers who have missed the trail have created a path straight ahead. Continuing, the trail runs behind a fenced area on your left that holds living quarters for seasonal rangers off TN297. The trail joins an old roadway, and you'll begin a gradual descent.

The trail crosses an expanse of sandstone at 1.3 miles that signals your approach to the Laurel Fork Gorge. You'll soon bear

73

right off the old roadbed and begin descending steeply along steps carved into the rock. The trail then rejoins the old road to continue the descent toward Laurel Fork. At 1.5 miles watch for a rock step on the right side of the trail that indicates a right turn away from the old road. You'll pass through woods and descend through three switchbacks to once again meet the old road. This swing to the right has cut off a steep section of the roadway.

Continue your walk down the old road; you'll drop into rhododendron and level out to a trail junction at 1.7 miles with the Laurel Fork Creek Trail. To the right, the trail leads to the northeast. Turn to the left to head toward the Middle Creek area.

Almost immediately, you must ford Laurel Fork; the creek is wide and hardly ever is low enough you can rockhop. This is the first of 18 times you'll ford Laurel Fork, so be prepared. At times of high water, the creek may be impassable; if you are not sure you can make it across, and remember you'll have to do it many times, come back another day.

Once on the other side of the creek, turn left and walk upstream. You'll be walking along an old roadbed; for most of this walk, the trail off and on follows the old road. The walk is through the floodplain of the creek, sandy in places and shrouded in pine and hemlock and scattered hardwood. You'll cross several small tributaries. The occasional dense stands of hemlock along the way make good campsites, but not in flood seasons. The trail passes through stands of laurel for which the creek is named.

At 1.9 miles the trail curves left away from the old road into a hemlock grove and then curves right into a more open area that must have been a field at one time but is now overgrown in pine and brambles. The trail reconnects with the road and heads up a slope to a junction with an old roadway up to the right that is the proposed extension of the Salt Pine Trail. From here on, the Laurel Fork Creek Trail is for hikers only. Bear left here and walk down the road to the second creek ford at 2.0 miles.

Ford the creek four more times. At 2.6 miles, the trail veers left away from the road and crosses an oxbow of the creek that in low water is dry. You'll cross the other side of the oxbow before rejoining the old road. Ford again at 2.9 miles.

The trail then crosses a small side stream and passes through the largest patch of climbing fern we have ever seen. You'll need to watch through this section; the trail veers away from the road several times, crossing another small side stream along the way. You'll ford again at 3.4 miles; notice the rock bluff to your left.

The trail rejoins the road only to veer away again to the left to move along a secondary roadbed. At 3.6 miles, watch for where the trail turns off to the right to rejoin the original road; the turn is easy to miss. Ford five more times. At 4.3 miles, you'll cross a side stream in an overgrown area where the trail is not well marked. Follow what appears to be the most traveled path; you should soon see a blaze. The trail then passes through the boggy area of a side stream.

At 4.5 miles, you must drop into the creek, but do not ford to the other side. In a few feet, the trail comes out on the same side of the creek; you've just bypassed a slough on the east side. The trail then follows an island between two sloughs; notice the rock wall to the east with a wet-weather waterfall. The trail then curves left, back toward the creek, and at 4.7 miles turns left at a campsite to ford the creek. You'll ford twice more and then ford Laurel Fork for the last time at 5.1 miles.

Then at 5.2 miles, the trail fords Ben Creek, a tributary of Laurel Fork. At this crossing the old road you're on continues up the tributary, but do not follow it. Just on the other side of Ben Creek, you'll see the trail heading to the right up the slope. Pause for a moment to scan for a small natural arch at the top of the low ridge just ahead on the west side of Ben Creek. As you walk up the trail, look back to your left at the ridgeline.

The trail climbs from the creek in a moderately steep ascent. After a couple of switchbacks, you'll come to steps cut in the rock bluff at 5.3 miles. The steps can be slippery if wet. The trail then curves back left over the rock bluff. You'll see to your left the deep cove you were headed into before climbing up the bluff. At 5.4 miles, stay left where an old trail heads up the slope. You'll make a couple more switchbacks as you continue to climb out of the gorge of the Laurel Fork and finally come to a trail junction at 5.6 miles. You've now connected with the Slave Falls Loop. Turn left on the loop to make your way to the Sawmill Trailhead in 1.1 miles or the Middle Creek Trailhead in 2.8 miles.

23 Laurel Fork Creek Trail to the Station Camp Area 🚶🚶

6.9 miles one-way
Moderate
Elevation loss: 350 ft.
Cautions: Numerous creek fords impassable in high water
Connections: Salt Pine Trail 🚶🚶, Black House Branch Trail ∩,
Fork Ridge Trail ∩, Duncan Hollow Trail ∩,
John Muir Trail 🚶🚶

Attractions: Enjoy a walk along the Laurel Fork of Station Camp Creek.

Trailhead: Follow the directions in Trail #21 to the West Entrance Trailhead and then follow the directions in Trail #22 along the Salt Pine Trail 1.7 miles to the junction at Laurel Fork.

Description: The Laurel Fork Creek Trail to the left at this junction leads to the Middle Creek area in the northwest corner of the park. Turn to the right to head toward Station Camp.

At 0.1 mile, you'll reach the edge of Laurel Fork, which you must ford. In the next two miles, you will ford the creek 11 times. These fords can be dangerous in times of high water, so you should probably plan on doing this hike during dry times of the year.

As you follow Laurel Fork, crossing it several times, you'll walk through a bottomland of rhododendron, hemlock stands, small pines, and a variety of hardwoods. The trail is often sandy and often follows an old roadway. The creek washes up against sandstone bluffs. Small side streams cross the path to join Laurel Fork. In fall, the floating leaves of yellow and red create swirls of color in the slowly moving water.

At 1.2 miles the old roadbed you're on curves left down to the creek, but the trail continues straight to the seventh crossing just downstream. After the eighth ford, the trail becomes faint in an overgrown area, but stay generally left along the creek bank and you'll soon find the way open again. In a hemlock stand, watch for a boulder on the right that has several trees growing on top; a good campsite. Just beyond the boulder, you'll ford the creek for the ninth time at 2.0 miles.

Then at 2.8 miles, you'll reach a junction with the Black House Branch Trail for horses; if you try to figure out all the signs, you'll just get confused, so ignore them. You can loop back to the West Entrance Trailhead here by turning to the right where the horse trail fords Laurel Fork and heads up a road 0.4 mile to connect with the Jacks Ridge Loop. Turning right on the loop it's then 0.8 mile out to West Bandy Creek Road, where you'll turn right again and walk up the gravel road 1.9 miles back to the trailhead on TN297.

To continue on the Laurel Fork Creek Trail, stay straight on the Black House Branch Trail, which is the road that runs beside the creek. At 2.9 miles, the hiking trail turns off to the right while the horse trail continues on the road to the left.

Turning right, the Laurel Fork Creek Trail passes through a grassy area and then a hemlock wood to parallel Laurel Fork downstream and then to ford the creek at 3.0 miles. The trail crosses the inside of a meander of the stream, with good campsites in a hemlock wood. Camp in the floodplain of the creek only in dry seasons. You'll ford the stream again at 3.1 miles.

The trail now heads downstream to then climb to the left. The trail stays on this northwest side of Laurel Fork, moving up and down, crossing side drainages, passing large hemlocks, white pines, and beeches. You'll pass around a large boulder to the left, and then you should watch for a switchback right and left soon after at 3.7 miles. You'll pass between two boulders and by a huge white pine on the left and then descend, turning right and left at 3.8 miles. The trail curves left up a cove to cross a rhododendron-filled side creek at 4.0 miles. Two more times, you'll make right and left turns as the trail works its way upstream. At 4.6 miles, you'll curve left around a moss-covered block of stone.

At 5.0 miles the trail joins a road to the left. You'll pass through an area of large pines. You'll lose the trace of the roadway for a time. Watch for an area where trees grow on top of rocks on both sides of the trail. You'll be back on the roadway again. Then listen for falling water in the creek below where a nice little waterfall beckons; watch for a block of stone on the right beside the trail at 5.2 miles and on the far side a 50-yard path down to a precarious overlook where a jumble of house-size boulders constrict the stream to a six-foot, two-step spout.

At 5.6 miles, the trail leaves the old roadbed to the left, but soon rejoins. Then at 5.7 miles, watch for where the trail leaves the road to the left; at the turn you'll see a medium-sized birch standing on its roots; it once grew atop a fallen log that has since decomposed.

The trail descends to cross a drainage on stepping stones and then passes along the edge of the creek and joins an old road at 6.0 miles. To the right, the road descends to ford Laurel Fork. Bear left on the road.

You'll pass through a hemlock wood and then at 6.4 miles enter a more open area of grown-up fields that were part of the subsistence community around the confluence of Laurel Fork and Station Camp Creek.

The trail passes through a wooded area and then more old fields to cross a small side stream and reach a junction at 6.7 miles with the Fork Ridge Trail coming in from the left. Both the horse and hiking trails now coincide along the old road paralleling the creek to a junction at 6.9 miles with the Duncan Hollow Trail fording Laurel Fork from the right and the John Muir Trail crossing the creek from the right on a high bridge. Station Camp Creek is just beyond on the JMT.

Falls on Laurel Fork

24 **West Bandy Creek Loop** 🚵

4.2 miles
Difficult
Elevation change: 160 ft.
Cautions: Not for beginners, steep and narrow sections,
creek ford
Connections: None

Attractions: The bike trail off West Bandy Creek Road presents challenges for the experienced mountain biker.

Trailhead: Follow the directions in Trail #21 to the West Entrance Trailhead.

Description: From the West Entrance Trailhead parking area, ride back out onto TN297; turn west and then turn right on West Bandy Creek Road. At 0.7 mile, watch for a bike trail sign on the left that marks the beginning of the mountain bike trail. At this writing, the trail has not yet been blazed, but you'll find blue flags occasionally marking the route.

As you head left into the woods the trail narrows and curves left downhill. At 0.9 mile the trail switchbacks right at a low bluff. Soon after, you'll connect with an old road; right will take you out to West Bandy Creek Road. Turn left on the road, and in a few yards turn right off the road. You'll soon encounter a steep downhill section and a steep uphill. At 1.2 miles, you'll ride across bare rock with pines and reindeer moss and then encounter another steep down and up.

At 1.3 miles, you'll join the faint trace of an old road to turn right and connect with another road. Turn right and then turn left off that road. You'll drop into another steep downhill at 1.4 miles, this time down bare rock. Curve right at the bottom and emerge onto an old road at 1.5 miles; again turning right will take you out to West Bandy Creek Road. Turn left and then watch for a right turn off the road at 1.6 miles. You'll soon begin a downhill section with a right turn into a steep descent into a cove and join another old road at 1.7 miles. Turn left here to ford a small creek and bear right uphill to a right turn. Follow the road you are now on into a steep ascent.

At 1.8 miles, at the top of the ascent, you'll connect with another road. Here you'll turn right and emerge on West Bandy Creek Road. Turn left; at 2.4 miles you'll see the bike trail turning left back into the woods along an old roadway.

The old road curves left, and then you'll bear left off the road to join another road to the right. At 2.5 miles, the trail turns right off the road, and you'll curve down the slope to cross a drainage at 2.6 miles. The trail then ascends out of the cove, bearing right.

The trail joins an old roadway headed north, until at 2.9 miles you'll stay straight on a side road as the road you're on curves right. Soon after, you'll cross the top part of the Y of an old roadway, bearing right up the left branch, to emerge on West Bandy Creek Road at 3.1 miles.

Turn right to complete the loop back to the trailhead. You'll reach the beginning of the bike trail on the right at 4.1 miles and then emerge back on TN297 and turn left back to the West Entrance Trailhead at 4.8 miles.

25 Gar Blevins/North White Oak Overlook Trails ∩

3.9 miles one-way
Moderate
Elevation loss: 140 ft.
Cautions: Loose gravel
Connections: Groom Branch Trail ∩, North White
Oak Loop ∩

Attractions: This ride follows the old Gar Blevins Road and the Narrows Road for the shortest access to the North White Oak Creek Overlook.

Trailhead: The old road begins on the south side of TN297 2.9 miles west of the Bandy Creek Road or 1.0 mile east of the West Entrance parking area. You can park at the West Entrance Trailhead and ride a bike east on TN297 to get to the Gar Blevins Trail; follow the directions in Trail #21 to the trailhead. Or you can start at the beginning of the road; the first few yards of the road are paved, so you can pull in and park to the side so that you do not block access.

Description: Follow the old Gar Blevins Road into the woods; you'll reach a junction at 0.1 mile with the Groom Branch Trail, which provides access to the North White Oak Loop to the east in 70 yards and the Gernt Trail to the west. Continue straight. At 0.3 mile the road crosses the upper part of the North White Oak Loop and from here cuts through the middle of the loop.

A section of the trail has been improved recently so you'll encounter gravel where there used to be ruts and rock ledges. You'll see side roads along the way, but stay with the main road.

You'll reach a road fork at 0.7 mile; the right fork is no longer used, so stay left through a field that can get overgrown with blackberry briers in summer. Soon the two forks come back together, and the road continues through the forest. You'll cross the Scott State Forest boundary at 1.2 miles.

82

At 1.5 miles, the road curves right and comes to another fork. The road to the right travels down to cross the west side of the North White Oak Loop in 0.3 mile. Bear left to stay on the Gar Blevins Trail. You'll reach another fork at 2.0 miles with the Gar Blevins Road to the left, but the Gar Blevins Trail takes the right fork now following the Narrows Road that eventually extends out a narrow point of land. At 2.1 miles you cross the state forest boundary again.

The road crosses the lower part of the North White Oak Loop at 2.3 miles and continues straight, headed for the overlook. The part of the road out to the overlook has been proposed to be called the "North White Oak Overlook Trail." You'll make a long steep ascent to the top of a knoll at 2.8 miles where vehicle traffic will stop when the road is improved. From here, you'll then have a couple of descents to hitching rails for the overlook at 3.9 miles. Just before this end of the trail, you'll see a road left that is blazed for an old horse trail that was at one time an alternative route; the path swings around and rejoins the main trail 0.1 mile back up the road.

At the hitching rails leave horses and bikes, and walk 30 yards up to a long flight of stairs that takes you on a ridge of rock that leads 60 yards out to the overlook. You'll have a good view of the North White Oak Creek Gorge; you can even see a patch of the creek below as it flows east toward the river. The O&W Railroad once ran along the north side of the creek, but trees shroud the old railbed so you can't see it.

From here, return to your starting point. Or you can take the North White Oak Loop east or west for longer return routes.

26 Groom Branch Trail ∩

2.4 miles one-way
Easy
Elevation change: 120 ft.
Cautions: None
Connections: Gar Blevins Trail ∩, North White Oak Loop ∩,
Gernt Trail ∩

Attractions: This horse trail serves to connect the Gar Blevins Trail and the North White Oak Loop with the Gernt Trail.

Trailhead: Follow the directions in Trail #25 to the beginning of the Gar Blevins Trail. A few yards down the trail, you'll find a junction with the Groom Branch Trail. To the left, the trail leads 70 yards to connect with the North White Oak Creek Loop to provide access for horses from that trail. Turn right.

Description: Headed west on the Groom Branch Trail, you'll swing through the head of a cove where the drainage passes under the road in a culvert. At 0.5 mile, you'll intersect with a road that leads 0.1 mile to the right out to TN297. Turn left to continue on the Groom Branch Trail.

You'll descend to cross Groom Branch at 1.2 miles; the stream passes under the road in a culvert. Up from the creek, the trail turns right. After a level section, you'll make a steep ascent to a junction at 1.7 miles with an old roadway to the right that leads out to TN297 in 0.2 mile. This is the junction that will eventually be a connection with the Salt Pine Trail to the north. Make a sharp left here into a downhill section to continue on the Groom Branch Trail. You'll pass through coves with streams of water in wet weather passing under the road and ascend to make the connection with the Gernt Trail at 2.4 miles at the Cumberland Valley Trailhead that's accessed off TN297 beside the Hitching Post Grocery west of the park boundary.

27 Gernt Trail ∩

3.3 miles one-way
(Laurel Fork Gorge Overlook 2.7 miles one-way)
Moderate
Elevation loss: 560 ft.
Cautions: Deep sand, steep rocky descent
Connections: Groom Branch Trail ∩, O&W Railbed ∩ ⬲

Attractions: This old road gives access to the O&W Railbed and offers a grand view of the Laurel Fork Gorge.

Trailhead: You may eventually be able to access the Gernt Trail from the West Entrance Trailhead where the Salt Pine Trail is proposed to extend south across TN297 to intersect with the Groom Branch Trail, which then gives access a mile to the west to the Gernt Trail. For now, drive west from the West Entrance Trailhead on TN297 one mile to the Hitching Post Grocery on the left. Beside the grocery, turn left on the Gernt Road that has been upgraded for 0.2 mile to the Cumberland Valley Trailhead where the Groom Branch Trail comes in from the left.

Description: Ride from the trailhead straight ahead on the old Gernt Road past the Groom Branch Trail to the left. If the trail has not been improved, mountain bikers beware of long patches of deep sand. You'll also encounter some exposed sandstone in the roadbed.

At 1.0 mile, you'll pass an old homesite to the right marked by remaining yucca plants. The road crosses the trace of an old road at 1.3 miles.

At 1.7 miles you'll pass through a pine woods and then at 2.6 miles reach a fork in the road. The left fork is the continuation of the Gernt Road as it begins its descent toward North White Oak Creek; the way is blocked by posts to vehicle traffic, which may use the road to this point.

Before turning left to make the descent, keep straight to get to an overlook. In 0.1 mile, you'll reach the end of the road at a wide turnaround. Look for a path to the right that leads 200 yards down to an impressive overlook of the gorge of Laurel Fork of North White Oak Creek, bare sandstone cliffs and a ribbon of water below.

Back at the junction, take the left fork to descend into the gorge. The route is steep, rough, and rocky. Watch for low ledges in the roadway. You'll drop below a rock bluff and continue descending into a right curve and bottom out at 3.2 miles. You'll then continue on a level section of road with the O&W Railroad bed to your left until you pass between posts blocking vehicle access and reach a junction with the old railroad bed at 3.3 miles.

This area once held a mining and lumber camp run by the Bruno Gernt family, who settled the community of Allardt to the south of the park in the 1880s. Here coal and lumber could be loaded on the O&W trains that operated in the Big South Fork watershed in the first half of the 1900s. The trains picked up coal and lumber at several loading stations along the track and hauled them east to Oneida where the material was transferred to the Southern Railway and shipped out of the region.

From the junction with the Gernt Road, you can ride east to connect with the Coyle Branch Trail. Long-range proposals call for a continuation of the Gernt Trail south across North White Oak Creek to Potter Branch Road.

28 Laurel Fork of North White Oak Creek 👥 ∩ 🚲

3.7 miles one-way
Moderate
Elevation change: 250 ft.
Cautions: Creek ford, mudholes, unmarked route
Connections: None

Attractions: On this unofficial route, you'll get to see the gorge of the Laurel Fork of North White Oak Creek. This route should only be attempted by experienced outdoors people.

Trailhead: From the West Entrance Trailhead, head west on TN297 to the junction of TN154. Turn south toward Jamestown. In 3.6 miles, turn left on Darrow Ridge Road. In 0.8 mile the pavement ends. Continue down the gravel road, which begins to follow the boundary of the BSFNRRA on the left. At 1.5 miles from the end of the pavement, a dirt road to the left is the beginning of the hike or ride. Before you get there, the Darrow Ridge Road becomes very muddy; if it has not yet been upgraded, you'll need to pull to the side and park before the mud if you do not have four-wheel drive and walk to the left turn.

Directions: As you head up the old road, you'll enter a tract of land that has recently been added to the BSFNRRA with the help of The Nature Conservancy, which purchased 1200 acres to preserve it until the federal government appropriated the funds to acquire it for the park. It was important that this region was preserved, because the Laurel Fork contains some of the cleanest water that flows into the Big South Fork. This acreage is sometimes referred to as the "Willamette Tract" because Willamette Timber, based in Salem, Oregon, helped to secure the land for the Conservancy by acquiring it from another company.

The way to the Laurel Fork is not marked because there is as yet no official trail into the area; so it is possible for you to get lost. Pay attention to where you are going so if you lose the way, you'll at least be able to get back out. Although there is no official trail, these backroads are used by the local people. Watch for all-terrain vehicles.

At 0.4 mile you'll cross bare rock as the old road begins a descent toward Laurel Fork. You'll pass a side road on the left and pass through metal posts for no vehicles. The road then curves left. You'll descend more steeply down a broad rock slope at 0.6 mile. Watch for a path on the left that drops from the road to a large rock shelter. If you explore inside, you'll find that the structure is a natural arch in formation; toward the back, an opening has eroded in the rock ceiling. In time, the hole will widen, separating the overhead rock from the back wall.

The road descends steeply to a ford of the Laurel Fork of North White Oak Creek at 0.7 mile. On the other side, ascend from the creek. The road once went to the left but is now a gully; stay to the right up the slope; do not take the road to the right along the creek. As you continue to ascend, stay with the main road as you pass roads left and right. Most of these side roads connect; they are merely different routes that all-terrain vehicles have made getting up the slope.

At 1.0 mile, you'll top out to enter a clearing; to the right you'll see broken cement, probably the plugging of a gas or oil well. Continue up the old roadbed. At 2.0 miles you'll cross the boundary out of the BSFNRRA where you'll turn right onto a side road, which curves back to the left; but immediately turn right again on a less-used side road that heads back toward Laurel Fork. You'll soon reenter the park. Stay to the road and respect private property during this brief turn.

At 2.8 miles, keep right as the road forks, and at 3.1 miles, keep left at another fork. At 3.7 miles, you'll reach the edge of Laurel Fork Gorge where you'll have nice views into the narrow chasm. The creek meanders through this region, having created promontories projecting from both sides of the gorge that are nearly interlaced like shuffled cards. Locals call this "Sawtooth Canyon." You can explore left and right along the gorge rim; to avoid unnecessarily trampling lichen growing on the rock surfaces, stay with paths others have made. Then retrace your route back to where you left a vehicle.

Laurel Fork Gorge

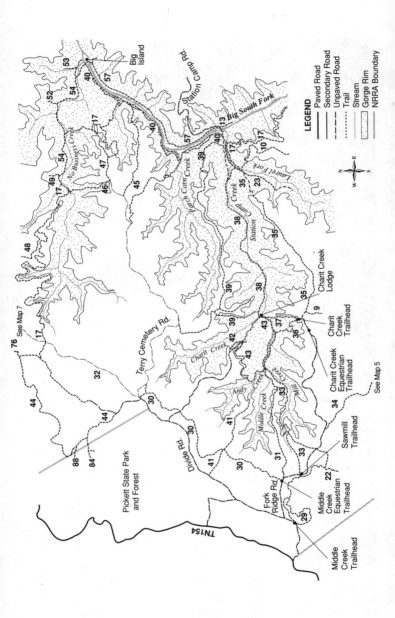

Map 6. Middle Creek
90

2⑨ Middle Creek Nature Loop 👥

3.5 miles
Moderate
Elevation change: 100 ft.
Cautions: Occasional stream crossings, boulder passages,
mudholes on last section
Connections: Middle Creek Connector Trail 👥

Attractions: This loop takes you by an impressive array of cliff walls and rock overhangs.

Trailhead: From Bandy Creek or the West Entrance Trailhead, drive west on TN297 to its junction with TN154; Jamestown lies to the left, and this will be your approach to the BSFNRRA if you come to the park from the west. Head north on TN154 from this junction. At 1.9 miles, before you get to Pickett State Rustic Park, which is just up the road, turn east on the graveled Divide Road; you'll see signs. The Middle Creek Trailhead and parking area lie on the right in 0.8 mile.

Description: From the trailhead sign, walk into the forest along an old road about 50 yards to a sign indicating the Middle Creek Nature Trail both straight ahead and to the left. To hike the nature trail clockwise, turn left into the woods on a footpath. This nature trail is planned for interpretation; so you may soon find numbered posts along the way and you'll be able to pick up a brochure that explains each point at the Visitor Center.

Along this first section, the trail parallels Divide Road. The end of May, you'll find blooming laurel. White-tailed deer bounded away at our approach. The Shawnees called the Cumberland Plateau "Ouasioto," meaning "mountains where the deer are plentiful."

The trail curves away from Divide Road to the right, and at 0.5 mile you'll skirt Fork Ridge Road that turns off Divide Road. You'll descend gradually and then more steeply with a few switchbacks to a junction at 1.0 mile with the Middle Creek Connector Trail that leads 0.8 mile to the Slave Falls Loop. From that loop, you can also access the Twin Arches, Charit Creek, and Bandy Creek areas in long hikes.

To continue the Middle Creek Nature Trail, bear right. You'll cross a stream on planks and curve right to a rock bluff on the right with the creek running along the base of the rock wall. The trail now swings out and in, each time nearing the rock wall, often where rock shelters have formed. You'll pass several of these rock overhangs forming hollows in the rock walls, some quite large. Most have a trickle of water running from underneath, part of the erosion that helped create the recesses. You'll easily cross these streams on stepping stones. Occasionally, the trail meanders under the overhangs along their sandy floors and through boulders piled in front of the openings. A recent rain will leave small waterfalls that drop off the lips of rock overhead. Watch for falling ice in winter.

Rock shelters are often habitat for sensitive plant species. Stay on the trail to avoid unnecessary trampling of vegetation.

At 1.8 miles the trail climbs through rocks and then descends to cross a small creek on a footbridge. You'll skirt the rock wall again with alum root, moss, and fern-covered ledges. At 2.3 miles, the trail crosses a boardwalk over a low area growing tall fern. Keep straight ahead when the trail crosses an old logging road at 2.4 miles. You'll reach another rock shelter at 2.7 miles and then ascend stone steps; notice up to the right a pedestal of rock supporting the ledge.

The trail curves right to ascend above the rock bluff and follow an old roadbed through the woods. When the trail links up with a dirt road at 3.1 miles, turn right. You'll have to skirt some mudholes along the road to complete the loop at 3.5 miles.

㉚ Gobblers Knob Trail ∩

4.5 miles one-way
Easy
Elevation change: 120 ft.
Cautions: Steep ascents and descents
Connections: Middle Creek Trail ∩, Long Trail ∩

Attractions: Connecting the Middle Creek Equestrian Trailhead with Terry Cemetery Road, this trail for horse-drawn wagons provides a route north not open to motor vehicles nor bicycles.

Trailhead: Follow the directions in Trail #29 past the Middle Creek Trailhead to continue up Divide Road. In 0.2 mile, turn right on Fork Ridge Road. Then at 0.9 mile turn left into the Middle Creek Equestrian Trailhead.

Description: The Gobblers Knob Trail straight ahead is the continuation of the road into the trailhead. The reason it looks like a road is that it serves as a route for horse-drawn wagons from here to Terry Cemetery Road and to Three Forks; no bicycle use is proposed. This is also the beginning of the Long Trail that traverses the park all the way to Blue Heron in Kentucky.

As you descend from the trailhead on the graveled path, you'll cross a clearing that's likely an old homesite. Back into the woods, the trail swings left into a descent and then curves right to bottom out where a stream passes under the road in a culvert at 0.2 mile. You'll see an old bridge to the left that was abandoned when the new road was constructed.

You'll then ascend from the stream and wind through the woods to descend to a ford of Middle Creek at 1.2 miles. The trail then ascends to a junction with the proposed Middle Creek Trail at 1.5 miles. Turn left here and take an immediate right to stay on the Gobblers Knob Trail.

The trail dips through a hollow and ascends past a low overhang on the left at 1.9 miles. You'll dip through another hollow and then cross under a powerline at 2.0 miles. At 2.2 miles, you'll pass a road to the left that leads up to Divide Road, but that route is not a horse trail.

The road now swings through several coves and eventually crosses the Twin Arches Road at an angle to the right at 3.2 miles. You'll then curve left into a steep, winding downhill. At 3.4 miles, the road curves right at rock outcrops on the left and dips through some low areas to ascend to a fork at 4.1 miles. Left at the fork leads steeply up to Divide Road at Three Forks at 4.4 miles. Right at this fork leads up to Terry Cemetery Road at 4.5 miles; turn right to access trails up Terry Cemetery Road. Eventually the wagon road will extend across Terry Cemetery Road and continue north to the Peters Mountain Trailhead.

⑶⑴ Booger Blevins Trail ∩

2.7 miles one-way
Moderate
Elevation loss: 560 ft.
Cautions: Steep sections, unmarked route
Connections: Mill Creek Trail 𝔐, eventually the Middle
Creek Trail ∩

Attractions: Horseback riders will someday have access from the Middle Creek Equestrian Trailhead to Charit Creek Lodge along this old roadway; only hikers can make the connection at this writing. This proposed trail should only be attempted by experienced outdoors people.

Trailhead: Follow the directions in Trail #30 to the Middle Creek Equestrian Trailhead.

Description: From the trailhead, go back out on Fork Ridge Road and turn left for 0.1 mile to the Booger Blevins Road on the left. This is a proposed horse trail that had not yet been constructed when we were last there. Eventually there may be a connector through the woods from the trailhead to the old road so you can avoid riding on Fork Ridge Road.

Turn on Booger Blevins Road and stay with the old road past traces of other roads to the left and right and through a couple of dips with mudholes in wet weather. The road is mostly level as it heads out along the top of a ridge; this section of the trail is open to motorized traffic, so you may encounter some four-wheel drive vehicles along the way. At 1.3 miles the road makes an obvious curve right. You'll reach the end of the road at 1.9 miles.

If the trail has not yet been constructed, the way from here will be difficult for horses and virtually impossible for riding mountain bikes, but hikers can do it with a little scrambling.

Drop off to the left, still following the old roadway. You'll soon swing right and continue out along a ridgeline. At 2.2 miles, the trail bears left off the ridge and descends, at first gradually and then more steeply. At 2.3 miles, you'll reach the point of a spur ridge where the trail swings right to skirt the point and continue descending, even more steeply. Watch for a switchback left in the descent where the trail turns off the spine of the slope and descends through a rock passageway. On the other side turn right to then rejoin the ridgeline.

At 2.4 miles, bear left off the ridge to descend into a hemlock grove and continue out another spur ridge. At 2.5 miles you'll encounter the end of a long sandstone block along the ridgeline. Bear left to make your way along the side through a hemlock thicket. At 2.6 miles you'll cross under a powerline and then descend steeply once again to the bottom of a cove where you'll intersect at 2.7 miles with the Mill Creek Trail that connects the Slave Falls Loop to the right with the Twin Arches/Charit Creek Loop just to the left across two footbridges over Middle Creek.

Horses and bikes are not allowed on these trails, so if you have made it to this point by riding, you must turn around and go back or continue straight on what will be a horse trail. Somewhere near this junction, the Middle Creek Trail, not constructed at this writing, will connect with the Booger Blevins Trail. From this junction, the Middle Creek Trail will continue toward Charit Creek Lodge, following an old roadbed. The trail fords Mill Creek and follows Station Camp Creek downstream to connect with the Charit Creek Lodge Trail in another 1.2 miles.

㉜ Long Trail ∩

25.8 miles one-way
Moderate
Elevation change: 900 ft.
Cautions: Creek and river fords
Connections: Gobblers Knob Trail ∩, Middle Creek Trail ∩,
John Muir Trail 𝕸, John Muir Overlook𝕸∩♿, Stoopin' Oak
Trail ∩, Mark Branch Trail 𝕸, Sheltowee Trace 𝕸, Difficulty
Creek Trail ∩, Cat Ridge Trail ∩, Kentucky Trail 𝕸, Laurel
Branch Trail ∩

Attractions: This combination of horse trails makes for a long ride through the northern region of the park.

Trailhead: Follow the directions in Trail #30 to the Middle Creek Equestrian Trailhead.

Description: The Long Trail probably will eventually lose its designation in favor of describing the pieces that make it up as separate trails. But at this writing, you'll still see occasional signs for the Long Trail.

From the Middle Creek Equestrian Trailhead, head north up the Gobblers Knob Trail (see Trail #30). At 4.1 miles you'll reach a fork. To the right you can reach Terry Cemetery Road and turn right to ride an alternative loop of the Long Trail—turning on the Hatfield Ridge Trail to the Hatfield Ridge Loop and descending to Charit Creek Lodge and then taking the Charit Creek Lodge Trail up to Fork Ridge Road, which you'll ride west to complete a 13.3-mile loop back to the trailhead.

To continue the Long Trail north, stay to the left when the wagon road forks, and you'll emerge on Divide Road at 4.4 miles at Three Forks. Now head north on Divide Road. At 6.3 miles the John Muir Trail crosses the road. At 7.5 miles, you'll cross the state line into Kentucky; Divide Road has become the Peters Mountain Road, and the Daniel Boone National Forest borders the road on the left while the BSFNRRA borders the road on the right.

At 8.3 miles, an unmarked road on the right leads toward the John Muir Overlook. At 9.1 miles, you'll pass Forest Development Road (FDR) 6300 on the left. Then at 9.6 miles, you'll pass the proposed Stoopin Oak Trail on the right that leads down to the No Business Creek area. At 10.1 miles, the road passes FDR6105 on the left, which gives access to the Mark Branch Trail. Then at 10.6 miles, you'll reach an intersection with the Peters Mountain Trailhead up to your right. The Sheltowee Trace, headed west turns off the road to the left. Also to the left, FDR139 joins the intersection. Continue straight, now on FDR6101, which is the route of the Sheltowee Trace north; this is also the beginning of the Kentucky Trail. At 10.8 miles, turn right on Laurel Ridge Road, which can get quite muddy in wet weather.

The Kentucky Trail turns right at 12.3 miles on the Difficulty Creek Road. This is also an alternative loop of the Long Trail—down the Difficulty Creek Trail to connect with the Miller Branch Trail that drops to Big Island at the mouth of No Business Creek; you'll ford the creek and continue south on the Big Branch Trail, nearly impassable in wet weather in winter and spring because of mud, to connect with the Station Camp Creek Trail leading west to Charit Creek Lodge where you'll pick up the Charit Creek Lodge Trail to reach Fork Ridge Road and ride west to complete a 29.7-mile loop at the Middle Creek Equestrian Trailhead.

To continue on the Long Trail north, stay straight at this junction with the Difficulty Creek Road. At 13.5 miles you'll pass a road to the right that will be the Cat Ridge Trail leading down to the Big South Fork. The road curves left here; you'll pass a cemetery on the left and then turn right at 13.6 miles to stay on Laurel Ridge Road.

The road drops to cross a fork of Puncheoncamp Branch at 14.9 miles and then ascends. You'll eventually reach a graveled section of the road at 18.4 miles and leave the mudholes behind. At 19.5 miles, the Sheltowee Trace turns off to the left. Continue straight on Laurel Ridge Road.

You'll soon begin descending and pass a side road on the left blocked by metal posts at 19.8 miles. At 20.2 miles, you'll pass the Kidd Cemetery on the right and soon after encounter a massive rock outcropping called "Stepping Rock" on your left. The road continues along the side of the rock. At 21.1 miles, you'll climb steeply onto Stepping Rock; before the Forest Service improved the road, several ledges created steps up the rock. On top, the road curves right. You'll pass roads right and left and pass the old Bald Knob School at 22.6 miles.

Continuing on Laurel Ridge Road, now also called the "Devils Creek/Beech Grove Road," you'll enter an S curve and pass Bald Knob Road at 23.0 miles that leads right to the Ledbetter Trailhead. Future plans call for the horse trail to be rerouted down this road to the trailhead where you'll pick up the Dick Gap Trail, yet to be constructed, that will lead toward Blue Heron.

For now, continue up Laurel Ridge Road. You'll pass houses right and left and then turn right at 23.9 miles on Waters Cemetery Road, just before the Beech Grove Baptist Church. Before the Barr Cemetery, turn left at 24.2 miles on a new road that leads to Dick Gap Overlook; this will be the Dick Gap Trail. You'll pass on your right an old route for the horse trail, but keep straight until you'll reach the end of the road at 25.2 miles. The path to the overlook leads down to your left and is not open to horses or bikes; the view is worth the short walk.

To continue on the Long Trail, head into the woods from the end of the road on an old roadway. The old route comes in from the right. You'll pass another old roadway to the right and curve left in a steep descent to intersect with the Kentucky Trail at 25.4 miles; this is also the Catawba Overlook Loop. The hiking and horse trails coincide for a short distance before the hiking trail continues straight while the horse trail stays on the old road as it curves right in a steep and rocky descent. Future plans call for making the Kentucky Trail from here a multi-use trail to allow horses and mountain bikes to reach the west end of the tram bridge over the river to Blue Heron. Bikes will then be walked over the bridge, but horses must be tied and left.

Continuing down the road to the right, you'll pass below rock bluffs and an overhang to cross at 25.6 miles the lower part of the Catawba Overlook Loop, not open at this writing due to slides along the trail to the right. Continue descending steeply to reach a ford of the Big South Fork at 25.8 miles; attempt the ford only at low water. You'll emerge from the river at the river access ramp at the Blue Heron Community where you can end your ride or connect with the Laurel Branch Trail.

㉝ Slave Falls Loop & Mill Creek Trail 🚶🚶

Slave Falls Loop 3.4 miles
(Slave Falls 1.3 miles one-way)
Mill Creek Trail 2.3 miles one-way
Easy
Elevation change: 300 ft.
Cautions: Boulder passages
Connections: Twin Arches/Charit Creek Loop 🚶🚶, Laurel Fork
Creek Trail 🚶🚶, Middle Creek Connector Trail 🚶🚶

Attractions: On the Mill Creek Trail off the Slave Falls Loop, you'll find 60-foot Slave Falls and Needle Arch, and later on the loop, Indian Rock House.

Trailhead: From the beginning of Fork Ridge Road off Divide Road, you'll pass the Middle Creek Equestrian Trailhead at 0.7 mile and reach the Sawmill Trailhead on the left at 1.2 miles.

Description: From the trailhead, walk left paralleling the road 0.1 mile to engage the Slave Falls Loop at a junction. Turn right to walk the loop clockwise.

The trail passes through a mixed pine-hemlock-hardwood forest. At 0.3 mile, you'll dip through a hollow. Then at 0.6 mile you'll cross a fern-shrouded creek on a plank footbridge. The trail passes through another depression at 0.8 mile. At 1.0 mile, you'll get your first glimpse of the cove that contains Slave Falls. The trail soon after joins an old roadway and bears left.

The trail then drops through another hollow and up to a junction at 1.1 miles where you'll turn right to continue on the Slave Falls Loop. Straight ahead is the Mill Creek Trail. Just up this trail, look for a side path on the left that takes you 0.2 mile down among thick understory, over rock steps, and then along a rock wall through blocks of stone to an overlook of Slave Falls.

You'll find the slender waterfall splashing in a rock pit with a large rock shelter behind. The hard sandstone that caps the

Cumberland Plateau causes such dramatic geologic formations to form. Where water finds a break in the sandstone, it erodes the softer layers below, creating a waterfall. Erosion continues to remove the rock underlying the sandstone lip of the waterfall, hollowing out natural amphitheaters behind, as here at Slave Falls. The name of the falls comes from stories that runaway slaves once hid in such rock shelters.

Back on the Mill Creek Trail, continue up the trail to see Needle Arch before completing the Slave Falls Loop. At 0.1 mile, you'll turn right to drop and swing in front of the delicate natural arch with a 50-foot span at 0.2 mile. Again, it's the sandstone that makes the formation possible—only when the rock is very hard can such a thin ribbon of rock remain suspended. Erosion widened a joint to separate Needle Arch from the ridge behind; runoff and seepage removed the softer rock beneath the arch.

From Needle Arch, you can continue to 0.3 mile where you'll see an arch in formation, a small hole that may eventually widen to separate a span of stone from the rock wall. Continuing on the Mill Creek Trail, crossing drainages on bridges and then stepping stones and finally crossing Mill Creek that forms Slave Falls, you'll reach a side trail on the left at 0.8 mile that leads 0.2 mile to an overlook on the other side of Slave Falls. From this second waterfall overlook, you can then continue on the Mill Creek Trail all the way to Jake's Place on the Twin Arches/Charit Creek Loop at 2.3 miles; along the way, you'll cross several side streams spilling steeply down to join Mill Creek below and cross boardwalks over boggy areas, pass a junction with the Booger Blevins Trail, and cross two footbridges over Middle Creek to connect with the Loop.

Back at the junction of the Slave Falls Loop with the Mill Creek Trail, turn uphill to complete the loop. You'll follow a road lined with bluets in spring until at 1.7 miles the trail joins a dirt road. Turn left to emerge on Fork Ridge Road. Cross the road into the woods, and the trail soon joins an old roadway coming from the left.

At 1.9 miles, the trail follows a fork in the road to the right and then turns right onto a footpath. The trail now winds through the woods, crossing a bridge and several footbridges over drainages

Slave Falls

Indian Rock House
102

that are usually dry. At 2.2 miles the trail joins an old road and turns right to ascend past a left fork to a junction with the Laurel Fork Creek Trail at 2.3 miles. To the left, you can walk 5.6 miles with many creek fords to the West Entrance Trailhead. Turn right to complete the Slave Falls Loop.

The trail soon curves left where you'll see a path straight that you do not take. Twice you'll descend to curve left through a hollow before joining an old road that leads up to the Indian Rock House at 2.6 miles. Set in a massive rock wall up to the right, this is one of the largest rock shelters in the park.

After passing the rock shelter, the trail dips through a shallow drainage to a left turn off the old road; this roadway continues out to the Fire Tower Road above the Sawmill Trailhead. The trail now wanders through the woods, joining old roadways a couple of times, crossing a boardwalk in front of a low overhang, twice passing through open areas that were once fields or blow-down areas, to a junction at 3.3 miles. From here the Middle Creek Connector Trail leads left 0.8 mile to connect with the Middle Creek Nature Loop. Stay to the right at this junction; you'll cross Fork Ridge Road and close the loop. Turn right to return to the Sawmill Trailhead at 3.4 miles.

③④ Salt Pine Trail ∩

2.7 miles one-way
Difficult
Elevation loss: 360 ft.
Cautions: Unmarked route, overgrown, fallen trees, mudholes
Connections: Laurel Fork Creek Trail 🏃∩

Attractions: Although difficult because it is now an overgrown old road, this proposed horse trail will provide easy access from the Middle Creek area to the West Entrance trailhead. This route should only be attempted by experienced outdoors people.

Trailhead: From the beginning of Fork Ridge Road off Divide Road, you'll pass the Sawmill Trailhead at 1.2 miles and continue up Fork Ridge Road. The road forks; the overgrown right fork leads 0.3 mile to the site of an old fire tower where only the tower's foundations remain; take the left fork. At 3.4 miles, you'll reach Salt Pine Road, with room for a vehicle to park beside the road. At this writing, the trail has not yet been constructed and so the old roadway is overgrown and passable only to hikers who are willing to do a little bushwhacking. Eventually you'll be able to access this trail from the Middle Creek Equestrian Trailhead.

Description: Following the road into the woods, bear right around a berm; you'll pass a road on the right that parallels Fork Ridge Road. Continue up Salt Pine Road. You'll encounter trees down across the road if the trail has not yet been constructed.

At 0.3 mile, you'll pass the trace of a roadway to the left, and then the road you're on splits for a short distance to avoid ruts. You'll pass the trace of another old road to the left at 0.9 mile. You'll pass through a pine woods where small pines overhang the trail at 1.2 miles. The road ascends steeply to top a knoll at 1.5 miles where you'll cross another old roadway.

You'll descend to encounter a blowdown that blocked the road at 2.0 miles the last time we were there. Make your way around this obstruction to pick up the Salt Pine Road again and begin a steep descent into the gorge of the Laurel Fork of Station Camp Creek. You'll curve right and descend across bare rock and then bear left at 2.2 miles. The road continues to descend to curve right into berms that once blocked vehicle access at 2.4 miles. On the other side, you'll continue on a level section along the side of the slope before curving left into more descent.

The old road from here on had become so overgrown when we where there, the route was very difficult. If you manage to make your way down, following the trace of the old road, you'll bottom out and connect with the Laurel Fork Creek Trail at 2.7 miles. To the right is hiking only. The proposed horse trail route will turn left here up the Laurel Fork Creek Trail to ford Laurel Fork and reach a junction at 3.0 miles with the other part of the Salt Pine Trail that leads up to the West Entrance Trailhead at 4.7 miles.

㉟ Fork Ridge Trail ∩

4.0 miles one-way
Moderate
Elevation loss: 660 ft.
Cautions: Steep, rocky descent
Connections: Charit Creek Lodge Trail ∩, Black House
Branch Trail ∩, Laurel Fork Creek Trail ⚄,
John Muir Trail ⚄, Duncan Hollow Trail ∩

Attractions: This trail follows the old Fork Ridge Road east to give access to the Station Camp Creek area.

Trailhead: From the beginning of Fork Ridge Road off Divide Road, you'll pass Salt Pine Road at 3.4 miles and reach the Charit Creek Equestrian Trailhead on the left at 4.5 miles. You'll begin the ride here.

Description: From the trailhead, ride up Fork Ridge Road 0.1 mile to where the road curves sharply left; the Charit Creek Lodge Trail continues along the road to the left, while the Fork Ridge Trail heads straight into the woods on the continuation of the old hard-packed roadbed that was the eastward extension of Fork Ridge Road. Four-wheel drive vehicles are also allowed to continue east. A proposal calls for the relocation of the Charit Creek Equestrian Trailhead to this junction.

Continuing east, you'll pass through a junction of old roadways with an old animal pen up to the left; just stay with the main gravel road. At 0.2 mile you'll reach a junction with the Black House Branch Trail that heads toward Bandy Creek on the right. Continue straight on the Fork Ridge Road.

The road continues east through a pine and hardwood forest along the spine of Fork Ridge, the ridge separating Laurel Fork Creek to the right and Station Camp Creek to the left. You'll see an occasional old roadway off to the left.

At 2.0 miles, you'll see one of these old roadways off to the left as the main road curves left. At 2.3 miles the road heads into an S curve to get over onto this roadway that has paralleled the main road. You'll see another old pen on the left where a roadway drops off to the left at 2.5 miles.

The road curves left to descend below a bluff and reach the end of vehicle access at 2.8 miles. The trail continues along the base of the bluff, following the roadbed that now has soft tread.

You'll pass over a ridge at 3.0 miles with a roadway off to the right and begin a long, steep, rocky descent with rock ledges into Laurel Fork Gorge. It's best to lead your horse or walk your bike down this slope. A proposal calls for rerouting the Fork Ridge Trail off the road not far back to avoid this descent. The trail will then turn off left and descend to a ford of Station Camp Creek and connect with the Station Camp Creek Trail; so watch for this change.

In the descent, you'll curve left to continue down a small cove. You'll pass a jumble of boulders in the cove's drainage. The trail curves right and left to finally bottom out in a grassy area at 3.7 miles. The remains of an old chimney at a housesite stands on the left as a reminder of the subsistence communities that lived along Laurel Fork and Station Camp Creeks.

At 3.8 miles, you'll reach a junction with the Laurel Fork Creek Trail to the right. Stay left on the old roadway that parallels Laurel Fork downstream; here the Fork Ridge and the Laurel Fork Creek Trails coincide. At 4.0 miles, you'll reach a junction with the Duncan Hollow Trail that fords Laurel Fork to the right and then with the John Muir Trail that crosses Laurel Fork to this side of the creek over a high bridge.

The Fork Ridge Trail can be combined with the North Bandy Creek/Katie/Jacks Ridge Loop, the Black House Branch Trail, and the Duncan Hollow Trail to make a loop ride out of Bandy Creek of 14.6 miles.

Chimney at housesite

36 Charit Creek Lodge Trail ∩

1.5 miles one-way
Moderate
Elevation loss: 540 ft.
Cautions: Steep descent, creek ford
Connections: Fork Ridge Trail ∩, Charit Creek Trail ⅍,
Middle Creek Trail ∩, Twin Arches/Charit Creek Loop ⅍,
Station Camp Creek Trail ∩, Hatfield Ridge Loop ∩

Attractions: This horse trail follows Charit Creek Road down to Charit Creek Lodge.

Trailhead: Follow the directions in Trail #35 to the Charit Creek Equestrian Trailhead. Mount up here and continue east on Fork Ridge Road 0.1 mile to where the Fork Ridge Trail continues straight on the old roadbed of Fork Ridge Road while you turn sharply left to now follow the Charit Creek Road.

Description: Continuing down the gravel road, you'll pass parking for the Charit Creek Trail for hikers on the right at 0.1 mile. You must then make your way around a bar blocking vehicle access to begin the steep descent toward Charit Creek Lodge.

At 0.2 mile the road curves left in its descent and soon after curves right. Continuing the descent, you'll pass an old roadway on the left at 0.8 mile that will be the end of the Middle Creek Trail when it is constructed. The road bottoms out and fords Station Camp Creek at 1.0 mile. At 1.1 miles, the Twin Arches/Charit Creek Loop joins the road from the left. At 1.5 miles, you'll reach a footbridge over Charit Creek; horses and mountain bikes must ford the creek to enter the lodge area.

On the other side, you'll see the trailhead to the left for the Station Camp Creek Trail/Hatfield Ridge Loop. If you're staying at the lodge, do not ride horses through the lodge complex; turn right down a trail that follows Charit Creek to its confluence with Station Camp Creek and then turn down Station Camp Creek to follow the path to the stables at the far side of the complex.

37 Charit Creek Trail 🏃🏃

0.8 mile one-way
Moderate
Elevation loss: 500 ft.
Cautions: Stairs, steep descent, creek ford
Connections: Charit Creek Lodge Trail ∩, Twin Arches/Charit
Creek Loop 🏃🏃, Station Camp Creek Trail ∩,
Hatfield Ridge Loop ∩

Attractions: The trail leads to an old homesite that is now Charit Creek Lodge.

Trailhead: From the beginning of Fork Ridge Road off Divide Road, you'll pass the Charit Creek Equestrian Trailhead at 4.5 miles and continue up Fork Ridge Road. At 4.6 miles the road curves left. And then at 4.7 miles, you'll find trailhead parking on the right. The road, blocked by a gate farther down, leads all the way to the lodge and is used as the horse trail. The hiking trail begins at the far end of the parking area.

Description: You'll descend through a couple of switchbacks and cross a footbridge over a small drainage to reach a stairway at 0.1 mile that drops into the head of a hollow; a wet-weather waterfall trickles off the bluff to the left. Turn right at the bottom of the stairs, following the rock bluff. The trail then turns away from the bluff and descends in a forest dotted with large beeches. At 0.2 mile, the trail switchbacks left just before a huge decaying log lying in the forest. After a switchback right, watch for a boulder up to the right in the grip of a tree growing on top.

As you continue to descend down the cove, the trail makes several switchbacks. As the trail turns left to pass through large boulders at 0.6 mile, watch for stone crop, trillium, and rue anemone growing on the rock. Along the way you'll also see hepatica, chickweed, phlox, violets, cinquefoil, and more in spring. Once through the boulders, turn right.

Continue the descent with Station Camp Creek below to your left. You'll descend waterbar steps to creek level at 0.7 mile.

Then cross the floodplain of the creek to a ford over to the Charit Creek Lodge complex at 0.8 mile. At low water you can step on boulders in the creekbed. Just before the creek crossing, you'll see Charit Creek joining Station Camp Creek on the other side.

Charit Creek Lodge consists of several structures: a large central building with two cabins to the right and a solar bath-house to the rear. An old barn stands to the left, and a corncrib, now used as a residence, sits in front. The lodge operates as a concession. You can get meals with your lodging; reservations are needed. This is also a favorite place for horse riders who can leave their horses in the stables to the far right.

The Charit Creek/Station Camp area was once the home of Jonathan Blevins, one of the early settlers. He came with his family to the region in the late 1700s and later moved to this area sometime in the 1850s. The main lodge building incorporates an old cabin, built around 1816, that Blevins could have used as the home for his family. Some locals speculate that he may have lived a mile and a half farther down Station Camp Creek at the housesite near where he is buried in the Hatfield Cemetery. He died in 1863 from bee stings.

Later, others lived at Charit Creek—Jonathan Burke and William Riley Hatfield, both of whom lie in a small cemetery just east of the lodge complex in the open area above the stables, and Oscar Blevins with his father John, who were descendants of Jonathan Blevins and who built the present barn, corncrib, and a blacksmith shop behind the lodge. The last family to live here, the Phillips, sold the homesite to Joe Simpson around 1963, who operated it as the Parch Corn Hunting Lodge until 1982; Simpson brought in logs from other cabins in the area to expand the main building and erect the two outlying cabins. When the complex was purchased for the park, it operated as a hostel and was renamed "Charit Creek," after the creek that flows beside the lodge into Station Camp Creek that passes in front. Later, the buildings were converted to a lodge.

If you walk to the left after entering the lodge area, you'll find a bridge across Charit Creek that connects with the Twin Arches/Charit Creek Loop. On the lodge side of the creek, you'll also see a junction for horse trails. The Station Camp Creek Trail/Hatfield Ridge Loop leads to the right.

Charit Creek Lodge

㊳ Station Camp Creek Trail ∩

4.1 miles one-way
Moderate
Elevation loss: 130 ft.
Cautions: Several creek fords
Connections: Charit Creek Lodge Trail ∩, Charit Creek
Trail ⅍, Twin Arches/Charit Creek Loop ⅍, Hatfield Ridge
Loop ∩, Duncan Hollow Trail ∩, John Muir Trail ⅍, Parch
Corn Trail ∩, Big Island Loop ∩

Attractions: This trail meanders along Station Camp Creek Valley to the Big South Fork.

Trailhead: Hikers follow the Charit Creek Trail (#37) while horse riders and mountain bikers follow the Charit Creek Lodge Trail (#36) down to Charit Creek Lodge. At the back northwest corner of the lodge complex, you'll find the trailhead; at this writing a sign calls it the "Long Trail" because the Station Camp Creek Trail is used as one alternative for return from the Long Trail. To the left, across the footbridge over Charit Creek, you can also pick up the Twin Arches/Charit Creek Loop.

Description: Head up the road behind the lodge complex. An abandoned roadway that heads straight up the slope used to be the return route for the Hatfield Ridge Loop; because of erosion problems, the trail was rerouted. You'll pass a block wellhouse on the left to bear right and reach the newer junction with the Hatfield Ridge Loop at 0.1 mile; the Station Camp Creek Trail is the lower part of the Hatfield Ridge Loop. Continue straight on the old road, which is hard-packed gravel but eventually gives way to a dirt track with occasional mudholes in wet weather.

The road you are traveling once connected the various settlements along Station Camp Creek, which supported a community of subsistence farms in the 1800s and early 1900s. All that remain are the old cabins at Charit Creek Lodge, roadways, and a few cemeteries.

Continue down the old Station Camp Creek Road. You'll

descend to the edge of the creek and then ford a tributary stream at 0.9 mile. You'll see an old roadway up to the left on the other side. The road becomes sandy, and then you'll pass a huge boulder on the right with another roadway up to the left and soon after reach a ford of Station Camp Creek at 1.2 miles. This is the first of several fords, impassable in high water.

Ford the creek again at 1.3 miles at another huge rock. You'll find a good campsite to the right on the other side. Soon after, you'll ford again. At 1.4 miles, the trail enters the creek but then comes out on the same side. You'll ford at 1.5 miles. Soon after, the trail enters a clearing that was once a farmsite; a roadway leads off to the left. Stay straight through a pine woods and the side road rejoins the main road when you emerge from the woods. The road then curves to the edge of the creek and reaches a path up to the left at 1.7 miles that leads 50 yards to the Hatfield Cemetery where you'll find the grave of Jonathan Blevins, one of the earliest settlers of the region. He perhaps lived at Charit Creek, but more likely, he lived here, near where he is buried.

At 1.8 miles you'll ford Station Camp Creek again, but you'll also see a makeshift path to the left that avoids this and the next ford at 1.9 miles; please stay on the main trail. The road passes over a ridge. Creeks run under the road at 2.5 and 2.7 miles. Up the slope in this vicinity lies the Owens Cemetery near an old housesite marked by yucca plants; we were unable to find it.

At 3.2 miles, the Duncan Hollow Trail leads to the right down to a ford of Station Camp Creek and to a junction with the John Muir Trail. Continue straight. At 3.8 miles the Hatfield Ridge Loop turns up a road to the left. Stay straight, and at 3.9 miles the John Muir Trail crosses the road; the route to the left is also the Parch Corn Trail along this west side of the river. Stay straight and you'll made a muddy descent to pass an overgrown trail to the left; bear right to a junction at 4.0 miles with an unofficial side path to the right that connects with the Duncan Hollow Trail. Turn left to reach the mouth of Station Camp Creek and then bear left along the river down to the river ford at 4.1 miles. Attempt the ford only at low water; you must skirt a section of big rocks instead of making the ford straight across; if you cannot see the river bottom, you should probably not try it. On the other side, you can connect with the Big Island Loop.

On the gravestone:

JONATHAN BLEVINS
BORN VA. 1779 — DIED 1863
LONG HUNTER — PIONEER
1. KATY TROXEL — 2. SARAH MINTON
ERECTED 1976 BY HIS DESCENDANTS

Grave of Jonathan Blevins

114

㊴ Hatfield Ridge Loop ∩

9.9 miles
(Charit Creek Overlook 2.1 miles one-way clockwise)
Moderate
Elevation change: 500 ft.
Cautions: Creek fords, steep ascent and descent
Connections: Twin Arches/Charit Creek Loop 🚶, Station
Camp Creek Trail ∩, Duncan Hollow Trail ∩,
Hatfield Ridge Trail ∩

Attractions: This loop, which includes the Station Camp Creek Trail, offers a good ride with an overlook of Station Camp Creek Valley and Charit Creek Lodge.

Trailhead: Follow the directions in Trail #38 to the trailhead behind the Charit Creek Lodge and the beginning of the Station Camp Creek Trail. Hikers can access the Twin Arches/Charit Creek Loop across the bridge over Charit Creek to the left.

Description: To ride or hike counterclockwise, follow the old road east that is the Station Camp Creek Trail (see Trail #38). You'll pass the return of the Hatfield Ridge Loop at 0.1 mile on the left, and continue on the Station Camp Creek Trail with several fords to pass the Duncan Hollow Trail to the right and reach the junction with the far end of the Hatfield Ridge Loop at 3.8 miles.

Turn left up the steep road to continue the Hatfield Ridge Loop. The road levels off as it circles the end of Hatfield Ridge; you'll encounter an occasional mudhole. At 4.4 miles the trail turns left up a cove on the north side of Hatfield Ridge; you'll soon begin ascending the flank of the ridge. At 4.5 miles, the road switchbacks left in the ascent and soon after switchbacks right. As you near the top of the ridge, you'll see rock bluffs up to the left. You'll switchback left again and curve right at the point of the ridge to reach the top at 4.7 miles.

The trail now heads west along the ridgeline with some up and down, but mostly level and mostly a graveled roadway. In summer, watch for patches of blueberries on the floor of the mixed pine, hardwood, laurel forest. At 7.2 miles, you'll skirt the head of a hollow to the right. Then at 7.4 miles, you'll pass a no-vehicle sign to stop motorized traffic coming from the other direction.

At 8.5 miles, you'll reach a junction with a side trail left that leads 0.7 miles out to the Charit Creek/Station Camp Overlook. Turning down this side road, you must skirt some mudholes to make your way out this lobe of the ridge. Near the end, you'll pass hitching rails where horses should be left. The overlook gives you a good view of Station Camp Creek Valley and Charit Creek Lodge. Continue heading west from this side trail.

You'll reach a Y junction at 8.8 miles. To the right is the 1.1- mile Hatfield Ridge Trail following an old roadway to the Terry Cemetery Road at Gobblers Knob. Stay straight and then turn left to begin the descent to Charit Creek Lodge; you'll pass through posts blocking vehicle access. The descent becomes more steep and soon a shallow creek crosses the roadway at 9.4 miles with a dripping waterfall to the left. You'll pass a low over-hang along a rock wall on the left as you descend into a forest of large beech trees. The tributary of Charit Creek you're fol-lowing drops rapidly, with spillways in the creekbed.

At 9.5 miles, you'll reach a junction with the abandoned route straight; turn left along the new route. The trail is level at first, but then once more descends in a beech forest to a junction with the Station Camp Creek Trail at 9.8 miles. Turn right to get back to the Charit Creek Lodge at 9.9 miles. The entire loop from the lodge, including going out to Charit Creek Overlook is 11.3 miles.

④⓪ Parch Corn/
Big Branch Trails ∩

4.4 miles one-way
Easy to Difficult
Mostly level
Cautions: Creek fords, muddy in spring
Connections: Station Camp Creek Trail ∩, John Muir Trail 🚶,
Big Island Loop ∩, Watson Cemetery Trail ∩,
No Business Trail ∩

Attractions: This horse trail follows the old road along the river that once connected the Station Camp and No Business Communities.

Trailhead: This trail begins near the end of the Station Camp Creek Trail; see Trail #38 for details. You can also access the trail from the east side of the river off the Big Island Loop by using the Station Camp Crossing river ford (see Trail #57 for details); ford the river only at low water. After making the crossing, you'll ride 0.2 mile up the Station Camp Creek Trail to the junction with this trail north.

Description: The junction with the Parch Corn Trail on the west side of the river is also the junction with the John Muir Trail for hikers coming from the south. Both the horse and hiking trails then coincide up the old road headed north along the river. At 0.1 mile, the hiking trail turns off to the left but interweaves with the old road all the way to No Business Creek, so you may see hikers as the hiking and horse trails occasionally meet.

The trail stays with the old road the entire way. At 1.1 miles, you'll reach a ford of Parch Corn Creek and soon after reach a junction where the Parch Corn Trail turns left on the old Parch Corn Road. At 0.3 mile up this side road, you can reach the cabin built in 1881 by John Litton, part of the subsistence community that existed along Parch Corn Creek. Because this is a historic site, do not camp in the cabin or in the yard.

From Parch Corn Creek, continue up the old road, which is now the Big Branch Trail. You'll ford Harvey Branch at 1.4 miles. You'll cross other drainages along this road; they may be flowing in wet weather. At 2.0 miles, watch for foundation stone up to the left, remains of settlements along this road that connected the Parch Corn and No Business Creek Communities. The Watson Cemetery Road comes in from the left at 2.6 miles, now the Watson Cemetery Trail. At 2.8 miles, ford Big Branch.

Then at 3.0 miles, the John Muir Trail, on the slope up to your left, reaches a junction where it turns left up the slope. The Big Branch Trail continues north on the old road; an old hiking trail also follows this route. Watch for occasional piles of stone up to the left remaining from housesites and cleared fields. At 3.3 miles, you'll ford a small stream flowing toward the river.

The trail passes by large blocks of stone that have fallen from the rim of the river gorge. As you near No Business Creek the tread becomes softer. When you reach the ford at Big Island at 4.0 miles the tread is mostly sand and mud, well compacted in the dry seasons of summer and fall, but nearly impassable with spring flooding which dumps a lot of silt at this location. This section of trail may be rerouted or closed during the spring.

At the mouth of No Business Creek, you can ford across to Big Island in the middle of the river and then across to the east side to connect with the Big Island Loop. Ford only at low water. The bank on the east side is muddy also. You can also ford to Big Island and then cross back, passing upstream around the mouth of No Business Creek to pick up the No Business Trail.

From the river ford, the trail turns left up an old road, paralleling No Business Creek upstream. Near the river this road is muddy and so at first the horse trail goes up the bank straight ahead before making the turn left in order to skirt some of this mud. You'll see good campsites to the right, but camp in the floodplain only in the dry seasons. You'll soon rejoin the road as it continues up from the river.

The road passes over a low ridge and then makes a descent, passing an old roadway up to the left. At 4.3 miles, you'll ford No Business Creek. You must ford diagonally upstream several yards in order to pick up the trail on the other side and then connect with the No Business Trail at 4.4 miles.

118

41 Middle Creek Trail ∩

4.3 miles one-way
Difficult
Elevation change: 160 ft.
Cautions: Not yet established at this writing
Connections: Gobblers Knob Trail ∩, eventually the Booger
Blevins Trail ∩ and Charit Creek Lodge Trail ∩

Attractions: This trail will eventually provide access from the Gobblers Knob Trail to Charit Creek Lodge. This route should be attempted only by experienced outdoors people.

Trailhead: Follow the directions in Trail #29 to the Middle Creek Trailhead and continue north on Divide Road past Fork Ridge Road at 1.0 mile. Divide Road from here north is mostly a single track, so watch for oncoming traffic. You'll pass a gravel road on the left at 2.0 miles that connects with Pickett State Park. At 2.7 miles you'll see Middle Creek Road on your right. There's room for one or two vehicles to park without blocking the road.

Description: The Middle Creek Trail will follow the old Middle Creek Road east toward Charit Creek Lodge. This road was being worked on when we were last there; so by the time you arrive you'll probably find a graveled roadway. At 0.6 mile you'll intersect the Gobblers Knob Trail that leads to the left toward Terry Cemetery Road and to the right toward the Middle Creek Equestrian Trailhead. You'll probably find the Middle Creek Road upgraded only to this intersection; beyond, the route will remain an old roadway through the woods until the trail is established sometime in the future. But you can follow the old Middle Creek Road for a ways east along the ridge that stands between Middle Creek to the south and Andy Creek to the north.

At 1.4 miles a couple of old roadways lead to the left. You'll reach a fork at 1.6 miles; the left fork leads 0.2 mile out to a powerline where it deadends. The main road takes the right fork. You'll descend to eventually cross exposed sandstone to two posts blocking further vehicle access. The trail drops off to a lower level to continue following the old roadway. Although the path from here is too overgrown for horses or mountain bikes if the trail has not yet been constructed, hikers can have some fun; but do not attempt this route unless you are an experienced hiker and have along topographic maps and compass. Check with the rangers at the Visitor Center for the current state of the trail.

You'll continue along the ridgeline past thick carpets of reindeer moss. At 2.1 miles, bear right off the top of the ridge to stay with the old roadway, which rapidly disappears. At 2.3 miles bear left off the ridge in a steep descent out to the powerline.

Somewhere in here, the trail, when constructed, will continue down the slope to eventually ford Middle Creek and connect with the Booger Blevins Trail and the Mill Creek Trail at about 3.1 miles. The Middle Creek Trail will then continue, fording Mill Creek and following an old roadbed along Station Camp Creek to intersect at about 4.3 miles with the Charit Creek Lodge Trail, which follows the road down to Charit Creek Lodge. Until then, retrace your steps back to Divide Road.

42 Twin Arches Loop 👣👣

1.4 miles
Easy
Elevation change: 150 ft.
Cautions: Steep stairways
Connections: Twin Arches/Charit Creek Loop 👣👣

Attractions: The Twin Arches are two of the largest arches in the eastern United States, aligned nearly end to end.

Trailhead: From the beginning of Divide Road off TN154, you'll pass Fork Ridge Road to the right at 1.0 mile and the Middle Creek Road at 2.7 miles and reach a right turn on the Twin Arches Road at 4.2 miles. After turning right, you'll see the Gobblers Knob Trail crossing the road at 0.3 mile; you'll reach the trailhead at 2.0 miles.

Description: From the trailhead, you'll enter a mixed pine and hardwood forest with laurel lining the path and descend to a junction with the loop part of the trail at 0.3 mile. Turn left to walk the loop clockwise.

Soon you'll descend two sets of wooden stairs. At the bottom turn left and then right to stay on the trail. Another path continues along the rock bluff, but that is not the trail. At 0.4 mile the trail crosses footbridges over two small flows of water seeping out of the rock wall to your right. At 0.6 mile, you'll cross another footbridge over a seep and then reach the arch formation, approaching first the North Arch.

Twin Arches is the most spectacular geologic formation in the Big South Fork area. Nowhere else do you find two large arches so close together. North Arch has a span of 93 feet and a clearance of 51 feet. The Twin Arches/Charit Creek Loop passes under North Arch.

Continue to your left, past the stairway to the top of the ridge, to a trail junction on the left where the Twin Arches/Charit Creek Loop leads toward Charit Creek Lodge. Just beyond this junction stands South Arch, the largest on the Cumberland Plateau

South Arch
122

with a span of 135 feet and a clearance of 70 feet.

Both arches were formed by headward erosion, a process in which a gully slowly erodes up a slope, perhaps one on both sides of a ridge, until the sandstone at the ridgeline is reached. The sandstone resists falling apart, and so the rain and seeping water proceed to erode under and through less-resistant underlying sandstone, eventually opening a hole in the ridge.

Notice these arches occur in a very narrow spur of the plateau surface. This edge of the plateau is slowly receding. There was likely once an arch beyond the South Arch; if you explore to the south, you'll see a gap in the ridge with a mound in between that is probably the remains of a collapsed arch. As the slow process of erosion continues, the South and North Arches will also eventually collapse, causing the edge of the plateau to recede even farther. Other arches will likely form farther back as time goes on, probably where you crossed seeps emerging from the rock wall.

The Twin Arches complex also includes two tunnels. At the south end of South Arch, you'll find the West Tunnel, on the west side. The tunnel is 88 feet long and was caused by widening of a joint. A much smaller passage, East Tunnel, can be found on the east side between the two arches, under the stairway that leads to the top. Water moving through rock created the East Tunnel. Snakes are attracted to cool, damp places; take care.

Ascending the stairway to the top of the ridge, you'll see bare rock and patches of reindeer moss. You can then turn left along the ridgeline onto the back of South Arch. With some difficulty, you can then climb to a peak atop the arch from which you have wide views of the landscape. Take care; people have fallen from these arches.

From the top of the stairway, turn right to complete the loop, first walking across the top of North Arch. You'll ascend a steep flight of stairs that leads up a knoll. Passing across the knoll, you'll see a side path to the right to a viewpoint. The trail then descends some stairs. You'll pass another path to the right to a viewpoint and then close the loop portion of the trail at 1.1 miles. Retrace your steps back to the trailhead at 1.4 miles.

4̲3̲ Twin Arches/
Charit Creek Loop 👫

4.6 miles
Moderate
Elevation change: 400 ft.
Cautions: Steps, boulder passages, stream crossings
Connections: Twin Arches Loop 👫, Mill Creek Trail 👫, Charit
Creek Lodge Trail ∩, Charit Creek Trail 👫, Station Camp
Creek Trail ∩, Hatfield Ridge Loop ∩

Attractions: The trail loops by Twin Arches, rock shelters, Jake's
Place, and Charit Creek Lodge.

Trailhead: Four trails give access to the Twin Arches/Charit
Creek Loop: the Twin Arches Loop, the Charit Creek Trail, the
Charit Creek Lodge Trail, and the Mill Creek Trail. Follow the
directions to the trailhead of any of these and walk the trail to
reach the loop. The shortest route is to walk in 0.7 mile on the
Twin Arches Loop. Follow the directions in Trail #42.

Description: At Twin Arches, pick up the Twin Arches/Charit
Creek Loop under the North Arch; a sign directs you toward
Jake's Place.

The trail skirts the ridge, passing by several rock shelters
where in wet weather water trickles over the edge of the rock.
Flowers are frequent in spring; you'll find laurel, iris, and columbine.
At 1.0 mile, watch for an overhang where erosion has bored a
hole through the rock, creating a tunnel to the ridgetop, a possible arch in formation.

The trail loops south, leaving the ridge. You'll begin dropping into the valley created by the confluence of the three creeks
that form Station Camp Creek. At the lower elevations watch for
fire pink, fleabane daisy, dwarf dandelion, cinquefoil.

Finally you'll descend into a cedar bottoms to cross Andy
Creek on a boardwalk and stepping stones. Just before the crossing, you'll see a stack of rocks from an old homesite or from a

124

cleared field. At 2.0 miles, the trail enters the meadow and farm-site of Jake's Place. No camping allowed here.

The homesite probably dates to about the same time as the old log home that became Charit Creek Lodge. Several families lived at Jake's Place; Jacob Blevins, Jr., and his wife, Viannah, were the last. A grandson of Jonathan Blevins, one of the earliest settlers, Jacob, Jr., was known as "Jakey." He died in 1935, followed a decade later by Vi; they both lie in the Katie Blevins Cemetery near the Lora Blevins House at Bandy Creek.

Joe Simpson bought the old Blevin's home at Jake's Place and had it torn down and moved to Charit Creek, which at the time was a hunting lodge. The far bunkhouse cabin at the lodge is made from the logs of the house. Jake's Place is marked by a solitary stone chimney that has now toppled.

The trail continues through the meadow and soon reaches a junction with the Mill Creek Trail that leads right to the Slave Falls Loop; the waterfall is at a distance of 1.5 miles. Continuing on, you'll recross Andy Creek on a plank bridge, just above the confluence where Middle Creek, Mill Creek, and Andy Creek join to form Station Camp Creek. You'll follow the trail as it parallels Station Camp Creek downstream. Watch for cool wading pools in the creek. At 3.1 miles, the trail joins a gravel road, which is the Charit Creek Lodge Trail that follows the road down off Fork Ridge Road. Bear left to walk the road to the lodge at 3.5 miles. If you want to enter the lodge complex, you must cross Charit Creek on a bridge. On the other side, you can connect with the Station Camp Creek Trail and the Hatfield Ridge Loop to the left. To the right, you can walk to the front of the complex to ford Station Camp Creek and connect with the Charit Creek Trail for hikers that leads up to the trailhead off Fork Ridge Road.

From the bridge crossing to the lodge, the trail continues straight, first paralleling Charit Creek through a mixed hardwood forest. This is a good section for wildflowers in spring; you'll see bluets, cinquefoil, crested dwarf iris, violets of several kinds, chickweed, rue anemone, and more. The trail then climbs steeply with many log steps and switchbacks until you arrive back at the Twin Arches at 4.6 miles. You must then return along the Twin Arches Loop to the parking area for a total distance of 6.0 miles.

Chimney at Jake's Place

126

44 Rock Creek Loop 🧍🧍

7.5 miles
Moderate
Elevation change: 500 ft.
Cautions: Mudholes, steep sections
Connections: John Muir Trail 🧍🧍, Sheltowee Trace 🧍🧍,
Coffee Trail 🧍🧍, Rock Creek Trail 🧍🧍

Attractions: You'll follow part of an old railroad grade along Massey Branch as it drops to join Rock Creek.

Trailhead: From the beginning of Divide Road off TN154, you'll pass Fork Ridge Road to the right at 1.0 mile and the Twin Arches Road at 4.2 miles. At 4.7 miles, turn left toward the Hattie Blevins Cemetery; 1.3 miles down this road you'll reach the cemetery and the trailhead.

Description: Walk down the old road past the cemetery on your right, which contains graves of the Blevinses, Slavens, Burkes, and Crabtrees. You'll have to skirt mudholes along the way if there has been recent rain. At 0.4 mile the road forks, stay right, watching for the red arrow blaze.

The road levels out along a ridgeline where at 0.8 mile the trail turns right off the old road. This turn is very easy to miss so you'll need to watch for a path to the right.

Following this trail to the right, you'll begin a descent toward Massey Branch. After dropping into laurel and rhododendron, you'll reach a crossing of a side creek at 1.5 miles. The trail then follows Massey Branch downstream.

At 1.6 miles you'll reach a junction with the John Muir Trail to the right which crosses Massey Branch on a bridge. To the right, you'd reach Divide Road in half a mile.

Continue straight with the Rock Creek Loop now using the JMT. You'll see the blue silhouette of Muir as the trail blaze. The trail enters a gorge at 1.7 miles on a low ridge that is an old railroad bed left from coal and lumbering times. You'll cross old railroad ties and see scattered coal. At 1.8 miles, Massey Branch spills over a ledge to form a small waterfall on your right.

At 2.7 miles, the trail bears right off the old railbed and switchbacks down to a junction with the Sheltowee Trace National Recreation Trail. From the right the Sheltowee Trace has traveled south through Kentucky, passing through the Yahoo Falls and Yamacraw Bridge sections of the park, to then reenter the park and cross Massey Branch and make this connection with the John Muir Trail. Massey Branch has joined Rock Creek off to your right out of sight. All three trails now coincide to the left. Along with the John Muir blaze, you'll now occasionally see a white turtle blaze for the Sheltowee Trace.

The trail heads upstream, occasionally using the old railbed along Rock Creek. You'll cross footbridges and stepping stones over side creeks and encounter rock steps up slopes. A few times the trail turns up the slope and then drops back to creek level. Deep green pools in Rock Creek with sand and rock bottoms make great swimming holes in summer. The trail passes by several camping sites. At 5.6 miles, you'll reach a junction with the Coffee Trail. This side trail fords Rock Creek to the right and leads half a mile into Picket State Park and Forest to the Coffee Overlook at the end of the Coffee Road. This is also the Picket State Forest boundary; you'll see orange blazes on trees ahead.

At 5.9 miles, you'll encounter old rails and a train car wheel and just beyond, a junction with the Rock Creek Loop turning left. The John Muir Trail and the Sheltowee Trace drop down to ford Rock Creek and continue downstream on the other side of the creek.

To complete the Rock Creek Loop, turn left and make a long steep climb up the slope. Along the way, at 6.2 miles, the trail passes through a rock shelter. Continuing the climb, you'll reach the top of the bluff where the trail turns left. At 6.5 miles, the trail joins an old roadway and turns left. At 6.7 miles, you'll intersect with another old road; stay right. At 6.8 miles, the trail turns right onto another old road; watch for the blazes. You'll then emerge onto the cemetery road at 7.0 miles. It's now a half mile left down the road to get back to the cemetery and the trailhead.

45 Parch Corn/
Watson Cemetery Loop ∩

11.1 miles
Moderate
Elevation change: 660 ft.
Cautions: Steep ascents and descents, rocky footing, no blazes
Connections: John Muir Trail ♙, Big Branch Trail ∩

Attractions: This popular horse trail loop dips into the gorge of
the Big South Fork and swings by the John Litton Cabin on Parch
Corn Creek.

Trailhead: From the beginning of Divide Road off TN154, you'll
pass Fork Ridge Road to the right at 1.0 mile and the road to the
Hattie Blevins Cemetery at 4.7 miles. Continue up Divide Road
to pass on the right the wagon road down to the Gobblers Knob
Trail and turn right on Terry Cemetery Road at 4.9 miles at Three
Forks. Terry Cemetery Road is being improved at this writing,
and the work should be completed in 1995; if the work has not
been completed when you get there, you'll need to park at this
turn off Divide Road. This will add 2 miles one-way to your out-
ing. At 0.8 mile along Terry Cemetery Road, you'll see where
the Gobblers Knob Trail emerges. At 2.0 miles, you'll reach a
junction where the Gobblers Knob Trailhead will be located. A
fork to the right leads south to the Hatfield Ridge Loop. Eventually
a proposed Michigan Trail will turn north to lead to the Longfield
Branch Loop. Terry Cemetery Road continues to the left toward
the cemetery, but stop here to begin your walk or ride.

Description: From the trailhead location, ride or walk up Terry
Cemetery Road. You'll pass some old roadways and reach Parch
Corn Creek Road on the right at 2.5 miles. You will return, com-
pleting the loop, on this road.

Continue up Terry Cemetery Road, first ascending steeply,
to 3.1 miles where the Watson Cemetery Trail turns off to the
right on the old Watson Cemetery Road. Turn right here and pro-

ceed up the Watson Cemetery Trail. At 4.0 miles the road makes a short descent and continues out the ridge. The road narrows to a trail but still following the old roadbed.

Watch for where the trail bears left off the ridge at 4.3 miles while a less-used path continues straight. Descending, you'll curve to the right below rock outcrops. At 4.6 miles, the trail bears left off the road to swing around Watson Cemetery and then rejoins the road. After the cemetery, the road fades into the forest, but just continue on the path through the woods.

You'll soon curve left off the ridge and descend into a cove to cross a small stream at 4.8 miles. You'll curve right and descend down the cove. The trail makes a steep descent and then bottoms out at 5.2 miles to cross the John Muir Trail and connect with the old road along the Big South Fork that is the Big Branch Trail.

Turn right on this old road. Before reaching Parch Corn Creek, you'll cross six creeks and drainages along the way plus a few mudholes. The JMT occasionally comes out onto the road. Just before the ford of Parch Corn Creek, turn right up Parch Corn Creek Road, now the Parch Corn Trail. You'll merge with the JMT for a short distance to where the hiking trail turns off left on a bridge over Parch Corn Creek at 6.7 miles. Continue straight up the old road to where it skirts the creek so closely the roadway is often filled with water. If you're walking, you'll have to either wade or rockhop along the edge to reach the John Litton Cabin at 6.9 miles. Since this is a historic site, do not camp in the cabin or in the yard. A path down to the left leads to a spring.

Continue up the Parch Corn Trail from the cabin. The ascent is steep and rocky. At 7.0 miles, you'll cross a small tributary of Parch Corn Creek and then swing right to continue up the road. You'll cross the creek two more times in the ascent and finally reach the top at 7.2 miles. You'll bear right to pass through posts blocking vehicle access and continue up the road.

You'll see low rock shelters at 7.9 and 8.0 miles. The trail curves left at 8.4 miles and then emerges on Terry Cemetery Road to complete the loop at 8.6 miles. Turn left to get back to the Gobblers Knob Trailhead location at 11.1 miles.

John Litton Cabin

131

46 Longfield Branch Trail ∩

0.6 mile one-way
(4.1 miles one-way from Gobblers Knob Trailhead)
Moderate
Elevation loss: 500 ft.
Cautions: Steep descent, creek ford
Connections: Maude's Crack Overlook Loop 𝄃𝄃,
No Business Trail ∩

Attractions: This short trail descends into the No Business Creek Gorge.

Trailhead: Follow the directions in Trail #45 to the Gobblers Knob Trailhead and ride up Terry Cemetery Road past the Parch Corn Creek and Watson Cemetery Roads. At 3.4 miles, you'll pass Terry Cemetery on the right where the Roysdons, Slavens, Watsons, Millers, and others are buried. At 3.5 miles you'll reach Longfield Branch Road on the left blocked to vehicular traffic. A Terry Cemetery Trailhead is proposed for this location.

Description: Go around the barrier at the beginning of the Longfield Branch Trail. You'll descend along the graveled road-way down the drainage of Longfield Branch, a tributary of No Business Creek. At 0.1 mile you'll pass a small overhang on the right with a small pool in front. To the left, Longfield Branch runs down a ravine.

Continue descending, and at 0.5 mile the road makes a sharp turn left. You'll continue down through two more curves in the road and reach the edge of No Business Creek. Ford the creek at an angle to the left and connect with an old road that runs along the north side of the creek that is now the No Business Trail. The Longfield Branch Trail is the shortest route into the site of the old No Business Community.

A proposal calls for this trail to become a loop, turning left on the old No Business Road and eventually swinging back to Terry Cemetery Road up another old road.

47 Maude's Crack Overlook Loop 🚶🚶

2.8 miles
(9.8 miles round-trip from Gobblers Knob Trailhead)
Difficult
Elevation change: 260 ft.
Cautions: Unofficial trail, steep ascent through crack
Connections: Longfield Branch Trail ∩, John Muir Trail 🚶🚶

Attractions: Intricate rock and great views make this one of the more interesting hikes. This route should be attempted only by experienced outdoors people.

Trailhead: Follow the directions in Trail #45 to the Gobblers Knob Trailhead and ride up Terry Cemetery Road past the Terry Cemetery to the Longfield Branch Trail at 3.5 miles where the Terry Cemetery Trailhead will be located.

Description: Continuing up Terry Cemetery Road, at 0.4 mile you'll pass a road to the left. Staying straight on Terry Cemetery Road, you'll reach a side road to the right at 0.9 mile that's the beginning of the loop. Terry Cemetery Road continues straight where you can reach Maude's Crack in an easy walk, but for this hike you'll come back that way.

Turn right on the side road to begin the loop, you'll pass between posts blocking vehicle access and descend along the old roadway. You'll have to skirt some blowdowns since this is not a maintained trail. You'll drop below bluffs in your descent and then ascend to cross over a low ridge at 1.2 miles where you'll see a pile of stones on your left that appear to be the remains of a chimney; perhaps this was a housesite and, if so, a spring must flow nearby. You'll lose sight of the old roadway, which descends into the cove ahead of you.

From the stone pile, bear left, following a path along the base of the rock bluff. The path rounds a point of the bluff and heads up a cove along a wall of intricate rock formations. You'll pass by an overhang and then pass an alcove where rock has recently broken off revealing interesting patterns of the colored sand that makes up the sandstone. The path skirts the head of the cove at 1.3 miles and then descends to pass below a pink sandstone bluff before ascending to reach the top of a ridge and connect with the John Muir Trail at 1.4 miles.

Turn left on the JMT to continue following the rock bluff. The trail crosses a ridge below the point of the bluff and continues circling left to cross a saddle between the main bluff on the left and a sandstone knob to the right.

At 1.7 miles, the JMT switchbacks right to begin a descent into the gorge of No Business Creek. Just at the turn, you'll see a passageway to the left with two large rocks forming a portal. Turn left through this passageway and bear right along the bluff to walk up to where a piece of the bluff has separated from the cliff to form Maude's Crack. The passageway is named for Minnie Roysden, called "Maude," who once lived in the area; she's credited with discovering the shortcut she used when bringing lunch to her husband and other workers who were cutting timber in the gorge. The men couldn't understand how she made the walk from the house to where they were working so quickly until she told them about the crack in the rock bluff.

Now scramble up the narrow crack to gain the top of the bluff; be prepared for some scraped hands and knees. From the top of the bluff you'll have a grand view of the No Business Creek Gorge, Burke Knob to the right, and another sandstone butte to the left. Future plans call for a Maude's Crack Overlook atop this bluff.

From Maude's Crack, take the path that continues back along the ridge. At 1.8 miles you'll connect with the end of Terry Cemetery Road. Walk up the road to the right and you'll drop through a saddle and climb to a right turn on the road and then close the loop at the side road at 1.9 miles. It's then 0.9 mile back along the road to the Longfield Branch Trail and the proposed location of the Terry Cemetery Trailhead.

Maude's Crack

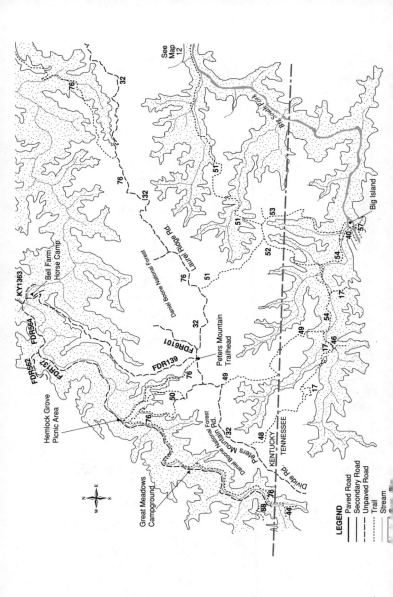

Map 7. Peters Mountain
136

48 John Muir Overlook 🚶‍♀️ ∩ 🚴

2.6 miles one-way
Easy
Elevation loss: 200 ft.
Cautions: Unofficial route, mudholes, steep dropoffs
Connections: John Muir Trail 🚶‍♀️

Attractions: At the John Muir Overlook, you'll have a sweeping view of the No Business Creek Gorge. This route should be attempted only by experienced outdoors people.

Trailhead: Continue out Divide Road from Terry Cemetery Road. The John Muir Trail crosses the road at 6.8 miles from TN154. You'll then cross the state line into Kentucky at 8.0 miles where the road serves as the boundary between the Daniel Boone National Forest and the BSFNRRA. Once you cross the state line, the road you're on becomes Peters Mountain Road. Watch for an unmarked road on the right at 8.8 miles, which is the Chestnut Ridge Road. Pull in and park; the road will be muddy after a rain so you may need to park somewhere else, like the Peters Mountain Trailhead to the north, and ride back to this location. This side road is passable only to four-wheel drive vehicles because of mudholes, and we've seen some of those mired down.

Descriptions: Head down the road, which runs along the spine of Chestnut Ridge. You'll pass a field on the left. At 0.1 mile, you'll enter the woods. Stay along the main well-traveled dirt road as you pass traces of old roads right and left. At 1.0 mile, you'll cross the state line into Tennessee.

The road bears right at 1.2 miles as another roadway heads left. At 1.3 miles, the road makes an obvious curve left where an old roadway continues straight. You'll pass another roadway to the right and reach a fork at 1.7 miles. Stay left.

After a time the road curves right and descends gently to a junction with the John Muir Trail at 2.0 miles. Posts block further vehicle access. Continue straight on the old roadbed, which is also the JMT; horses and mountain bikes may continue for

John Muir Overlook

138

awhile. At 2.4 miles, the trail turns down right off the road; here you must leave horses and mountain bikes and continue on foot. The trail drops with a couple of wooden steps onto a narrow saddle in the ridge separating Tacket Creek Gorge to the left and No Business Creek Gorge to the right. You'll then ascend up rock and wooden steps and bear right along the bluff to where the JMT makes a sharp switchback left at 2.6 miles. Straight ahead you'll see the bare rock bluff of the John Muir Overlook at the edge of the No Business Creek Gorge.

④⑨ Stoopin Oak Trail ∩

3.8 miles one-way
Moderate
Elevation loss: 600 ft.
Cautions: Unmarked route, mudholes, steep and rocky descent
Connections: John Muir Trail 👣, No Business Trail ∩

Attractions: This proposed trail descends into the No Business area and, until developed, should only be attempted by experienced outdoors people.

Trailhead: From the John Muir Overlook turnoff, continue up Peters Mountain Road. You'll pass Forest Development Road 6300 on the left and at 10.1 miles from TN154 reach Stoopin Oak Road on the right. The road is passable only to four-wheel drive vehicles, and those will have a hard time of it. Turn in and park to the right so you do not block the road, or if it's muddy, there's a turnout on the right just down from the Stoopin Oak turnoff. If you need more room to unload horses, drive on up Peters Mountain Road another mile to the Peters Mountain Trailhead and then ride back along the road to this turnoff.

Description: When the Stoopin Oak Trail is upgraded, you'll begin the ride at Peters Mountain Trailhead along a new section of trail that will link the trailhead with the Stoopin Oak Road. Until the trail is constructed, you can still make your way along this old roadway with only a little difficulty.

Head up the Stoopin Oak Road. You'll soon begin dropping below rock outcrops on the left. You'll see pullouts on the left that can serve as campsites if you've brought water. At 0.3 mile, as the trail tops a ridge, you'll pass another roadway to the left.

At 1.0 mile, the road makes a turn to the right where an old side road leads left. At 1.1 miles, the road splits; stay to the left to avoid the deepest mudholes; the way straight has become over-grown. You'll rejoin the original track at 1.3 miles. After a level section and some downhill, you'll reach a steep ascent at 2.0 miles. Once you level off, the trail passes rock outcrops along the spine of the ridge. At 2.2 miles, you'll see a path on the left that leads up into the rocks. The trail soon loops left over the point of the ridge. Tacket Creek flows in the valley to your right. The trail now heads down the other side of the ridge.

The road curves right into a descent at 2.5 miles where a side path leads left up to a rock wall and a spring with a pipe. The trail crosses the state line into Tennessee. You'll then reach an intersection of roads, which when we were last there was ob-scured by down trees. If the way has not been cleared, make your way around the obstruction and continue straight up the road; don't get off on one of the side roads. The road curves right on top of a knob. You'll drop to a small clearing where the road curves left at 2.8 miles to continue descending.

At 3.0 miles the road curves left to cross a small stream. The road continues straight and a side road leads left uphill, but you should turn right to cross a larger creek and pass through posts preventing vehicle access. You'll then descend into the No Business Creek Gorge. At 3.2 miles you'll pass through a tall rock pas-sageway to a steep, rocky descent as you drop below the rock bluff of the rim. The road eventually bottoms out at 3.8 miles to connect with the old road along No Business Creek. This is both the No Business Trail for horses and the John Muir Trail for hik-ers. Right along this trail will take you to the Longfield Branch Trail; left gets you to the Big South Fork at Big Island.

50 Mark Branch/ Gobblers Arch Loop 𝕩𝕩

4.0 miles
Moderate
Elevation change: 600 ft.
Cautions: Creek crossings, steep ascent
Connections: Sheltowee Trace 𝕩𝕩

Attractions: The Mark Branch Trail and the Gobblers Arch Trail combine to form this scenic loop, which drops into a narrow gorge and swings through a natural arch.

Trailhead: Continuing north on Peters Mountain Road from the Stoopin Oak Road, watch for Forest Development Road 6105 on your left in 10.6 miles from TN154. You'll see a low sign for the Mark Branch Loop. You can park here beside the road to begin this hike in the Daniel Boone National Forest. Or you might drive down FDR6105; in wet weather, you may encounter mudholes. At 0.6 mile along the road, the trail turns off to the right; there's room to park a vehicle beside the road at the trailhead.

Description: The trail begins on an old roadway blazed with white diamonds. You'll soon turn left off the roadway, descending to cross a shallow creek at the head of a hollow at 0.2 mile. The trail turns left to ascend up to a rock bluff. You'll follow the bluff and then drop through another hollow and ascend to a right turn on an old roadbed at 0.4 mile.

At 0.5 mile, turn left off the roadbed to descend along the bluff of a narrow gorge and then descend into the rock gorge to cross a stream on a footbridge at 0.6 mile; in wet weather you'll see a small cascade up to your left. As you switchback up the other side, notice the large hemlock sitting on a boulder.

You'll eventually begin a descent back into the gorge. At 0.8 mile, the trail turns right off the shelf you're walking and drops through the hollow and continues descending into the gorge. You'll switchback left in the descent and for a time follow an old railbed; the ties have decayed but left parallel depressions in the path. At 0.9 mile you'll cross a creekbed and continue descending to a junction at 1.0 mile with the Sheltowee Trace at Mark Branch. Turn left to continue the loop.

Along the Sheltowee Trace, you'll cross Mark Branch on stepping stones four times, and then walk in the creekbed to a bend where you'll climb above the creek. The trail crosses a couple of drainages and then emerges into an open area and a junction at 1.4 miles. The Sheltowee Trace turns left, but you can also follow a leg of the Trace straight ahead to a ford of Rock Creek in 0.1 mile to get to the Hemlock Grove Picnic Area. A bridge is scheduled to be constructed soon. You can access the Sheltowee Trace and walk the loop from this location on FDR137.

Back at the junction, continue on the Sheltowee Trace to a junction with the Gobblers Arch Trail on the left at 1.5 miles. The Sheltowee Trace continues straight to the Great Meadows Campground in another two miles.

On the Gobblers Arch Trail, you'll make a steep ascent of the ridge, finally reaching the point of a rock bluff at 1.7 miles. This point on the rim marks the confluence of the Mark Branch and Rock Creek Gorges. The trail swings left and stays along the base of the rock bluff on the Mark Branch side. Watch for patches of columbine in spring.

You'll pass a deep alcove in the rock wall, which has a wet-weather waterfall. At 2.0 miles, the trail heads up a hollow where you'll switchback right and ascend above the bluff. The trail now follows along the top of the bluff until you're back to the bluff point and then turns left to follow the bluff along the Rock Creek Gorge. At 2.6 miles, you'll reach a short side path to a vista of the gorge with the creek buried in trees below.

The trail follows along a low rock bluff and bears left to pass through Gobblers Arch, actually a low tunnel through the ridge, at 3.3 miles. On the other side, bear left to switchback up and walk out to FDR6105, not open to vehicles at this point. Turn right and follow the road out to a turnaround at 3.5 miles. Then continue up the road to the beginning of the Mark Branch Trail at 4.0 miles. If you walked in, you'll have another 0.6 mile back out to the Peters Mountain Road.

5️⃣1️⃣ Kentucky Trail 👫

26.2 miles one-way
Moderate
Elevation loss: 880 ft.
Cautions: Creek fords, mudholes
Connections: Sheltowee Trace 👫, Difficulty Creek Trail ∩,
Burkes Branch Trail 👫, Cat Ridge Trail ∩,
Oil Well Branch Loop ∩, Long Trail ∩

Attractions: This long trail provides for backpacking in the Kentucky section of the park.

Trailhead: Continue northeast on Peters Mountain Road from the turnoff for the Mark Branch Trail to an intersection with FDR139 to the left and 6101 straight ahead, at 11.1 miles from TN154. To the left, the Sheltowee Trace heads into the woods. On the right lies the Peters Mountain Trailhead, which can also be reached down FDR139 from the western end of KY1363.

Descriptions: From the Peters Mountain Trailhead, hike up FDR6101, following the same route as the Sheltowee Trace headed north. At 0.2 mile, turn right onto Laurel Ridge Road. In winter and spring the road can get quite muddy. You'll reach a junction at 1.7 miles. The Sheltowee Trace continues straight on Laurel Ridge Road, while the Kentucky Trail turns right on a side road that is also the Difficulty Creek Trail.

You'll reach a junction at 3.6 miles with the Burkes Branch Trail. Stay straight. At 4.0 miles, the Kentucky Trail turns left while the road continues straight. Turning left, you'll pass through posts and walk along an old roadway that narrows to a path and begins a descent toward Difficulty Creek. At 4.7 miles, you'll reach a short set of stairs. Soon you'll curve around a rock to the right and descend. Below a rock bluff at 4.9 miles the trail turns left; a side path leads to a ravine headed by a waterfall.

The main trail heads down the ravine to cross a footbridge over a side stream and switchback down to a bridge crossing of the main stream at 5.3 miles. This stream is a tributary of Difficulty

Creek, and you'll soon parallel the creek downstream. The trail crosses a footbridge over a side stream and then reaches a large bridge over Difficulty Creek at 5.8 miles.

Turn right and continue downstream. You'll cross a bridge over a side drainage at 5.9 miles and curve right to descend stone steps to a bridge crossing of a stream at 6.0 miles. Up steps on the other side, turn left on an old roadway. Soon the trail turns right up an old roadbed in a steep climb. Watch for the trail to turn left off the roadway at 6.1 miles. The trail curves around the head of a hollow and continues up the trace of an old roadway. At 6.3 miles, you'll bear right off the roadway and ascend to a junction with a dirt road at 6.4 miles. This road leads down from Laurel Ridge Road and is the proposed Cat Ridge Trail. Turn right.

The road heads out along a ridge and descends to where the trail turns on a path to the left at 7.0 miles. At 7.4 miles, you'll pass under an overhang and follow the trail up to the right.

A rock leaning against a larger rock signals a switchback left, but within a few yards you'll switchback right. At 7.8 miles, the trail crosses the trace of a road dropping steeply down the slope. You'll descend to emerge on an old road at 7.9 miles; turn left. Watch for the trail to turn right off the road in 40 yards.

The path descends to a bridge crossing of a stream at 8.0 miles. You'll then switchback down to a long bridge crossing of Troublesome Creek at 8.3 miles. On the other side, bear left up stone steps and switch right as you ascend from the creek. The path joins an old roadbed. At 8.8 miles, bear left to ford Lone Cliff Branch just above its confluence with Troublesome Creek. On the other side, go left through an overgrown floodplain and turn right. Soon, you'll reach an old road up to the left that will be the Lone Cliff Branch Trail leading up to the Sheltowee Trace. Straight ahead and up to the left will be part of the Oil Well Branch Loop coming down from the Ledbetter Place Trailhead; from here that trail will coincide with the Kentucky Trail to the north. Bear right off the road into the floodplain of the creek; you won't see much of a trail, but keep going and you'll find a roadway. Bear left to cross a small stream and turn right to a ford of Watson Branch at 9.0 miles. On the other side you'll pick up the old roadway and continue down Troublesome Creek.

You'll reach a fork at 9.5 miles; bear left. Continue bearing left as you leave Troublesome Creek and follow the old road north along the Big South Fork. At 9.7 miles, notice a huge block of stone in the river to your right, split in two.

At 10.0 miles, rockhop a streambed where a bridge has broken and scattered. After a little rise, the trail curves left at 10.7 miles, where you'll find off-trail to the right a pipe emerging from the ground that is the first commercial oil well in the U.S. In 1818 Marcus Huling and Andrew Zimmerman discovered oil here while searching for salt. At the time, oil had little commercial value, but Huling hauled some of the oil out and sold it as an ingredient in liniments. The well is off to your right about 50 paces. The original wooden casing has been replaced with the metal pipe. A post standing near the pipe is a replica of the brace for a long pole that acted as a spring in the drilling process.

A little farther up the trail, you'll see another pipe sticking out of the ground on the left, probably another well. At 10.8 miles, ford Oil Well Branch. The sign pointing upstream directs you to a broken-down bridge. The trail actually continues straight. Soon after, you'll pass a road up to the left that will eventually be the other side of the Oil Well Branch Loop. At 11.4 miles, pass around a boulder resting in the old roadway.

You'll reach a junction where the trail turns up a road to the left at 11.7 miles. The road along the river continues straight but soon gets overgrown. As you ascend left up the old road, you'll cross two footbridges over a drainage and continue uphill to pass through posts and emerge on the graveled Bald Knob Road at 12.2 miles. Turn left. At 12.6 miles, you'll pass the return of the Oil Well Branch Loop on the left; just up this road, you'll find the Hill Cemetery on your right. Continue up Bald Knob Road to pass the Ledbetter Place Trailhead at 12.8 miles.

At 12.9 miles, the Kentucky Trail turns right on a side road. At 13.0 miles, you'll pass the King Cemetery on the right. At 13.3 miles the road fades into the landscape and becomes a path. You'll pass through a hemlock grove and walk around the head of a hollow and descend to a road at 13.7 miles. Turn left to a bridge crossing of the south fork of Laurel Crossing Branch. On the other side, watch for the trail to turn off the road to the right. At 14.0 miles, you'll cross the north fork of Laurel Crossing

First Commercial Oil Well
146

Branch on a bridge. Keep your eye on the blazes through the next section that takes you through boulders and switchbacks.

At 15.1 miles, you'll reach a junction with an old road. To the left the overgrown road leads up to the back of the Waters Cemetery at the end of the Waters Cemetery Road. Turn right.

The trail soon veers right off the road. You'll curve left and reach an old homesite at 15.3 miles. The trail passes through the clearing and then bears left on an old roadway. The road ascends and the trail veers off to the right at 15.5 miles. You'll dip through an old roadway and emerge at a field. Walk straight across and you'll find were the trail reenters the woods. You'll emerge at another portion of the field; stay along the edge. At 15.7 miles, the trail turns right into the woods. Curve left to begin a descent at 15.9 miles. With switchbacks you'll reach a junction with a side trail to Big Springs Falls at 16.4 miles. From here the Kentucky Trail continues north to pass Dick Gap Falls and Catawba Overlook and reach the tram bridge over to the Blue Heron Mining Community at 19.8 miles. (See Trail #67 for details.) The Kentucky Trail then continues north following the old tramroad on this west side of the Big South Fork (see Trail #66).

At 22.1 miles you'll see concrete piers that anchored a mining structure. Continue straight up the road, following a creek upstream. You'll work your way up the cove, crossing the stream and a couple of bridges to reach the drier plateautop.

At 23.8 miles, the trail crosses a bridge over a creek and then crosses the trace of an old road. You'll pass under a powerline and emerge on Wilson Ridge Road at 24.6 miles. Turn right, but not up the side road. At 24.8 miles, a side road leads up to the Wilson Cemetery. Then at 24.9 miles the road passes a house on the left and the graveled part ends just beyond. The trail continues down the roadway, now a dirt track. At 25.0 miles you'll pass under a powerline. Stay left where the road forks at 25.3 miles. The trail turns left off the road at 25.5 miles.

Now on a path, you'll round the point of Wilson Ridge and begin a serious descent. With turns and switchbacks and stone steps, you'll descend the ridge to bottom out at a ford of Grassy Fork. Up from the creek, turn left and walk up to the end of the trail and a junction with the Sheltowee Trace at 26.2 miles. To the right, it's then one mile to KY92 at the Yamacraw Bridge.

𝟱𝟮 Burkes Branch/ Dry Branch Trails 👫

2.2 miles one-way
Moderate
Elevation loss: 680 ft.
Cautions: Steep descent
Connections: Kentucky Trail 👫, Difficulty Creek Trail ∩,
No Business Trail ∩, John Muir Trail 👫

Attractions: These hiking trails drop into the No Business Creek Gorge to connect with the John Muir Trail.

Trailhead: Follow the directions in Trail #51 to the Peters Mountain Trailhead and then ride horses or bikes or hike north up FDR6101 following the route of both the Sheltowee Trace and the Kentucky Trail. Turn right on Laurel Ridge Road at 0.2 mile and walk/ride to a junction at 1.7 miles where the Kentucky Trail turns off Laurel Ridge Road to the right. At 3.6 miles along this road, which will also be the Difficulty Creek Trail, you'll reach a junction with the Burkes Branch Trail, an old roadway to the right.

Description: Turning right on the Burkes Branch Trail, you'll descend past an old roadway to the right. At 0.5 mile, you'll cross the state line into Tennessee and pass through posts blocking vehicle access. Soon after, listen for a wet-weather waterfall spilling over a rock wall at the gorge rim to your right. You'll descend bare sandstone to dip through a saddle. Over the next ridge, you'll begin a serious descent into the gorge of No Business Creek. Somewhere in here a proposed side trail will lead to the Burkes Branch Overlook.

At 0.9 mile, a side road comes in from the left. Soon after, watch for a cascade in the stream to your right. At 1.0 mile, you'll pass massive rock that makes up the gorge rim. The old road descends steeply until at 1.2 miles you'll cross a small stream that is a tributary of Burkes Branch. You'll continue to descend to a junction at 1.4 miles where the Dry Branch Trail turns off on a
148

footpath to the right. Straight ahead a few yards, you'll ford Burkes Branch and pass through posts to connect with the No Business Trail that follows the old road along No Business Creek.

Turning right on the Dry Branch Trail, you'll pass through the woods with Burkes Branch and the horse trail down to the left. At 1.6 miles the hiking trail swings next to the horse trail to turn up an old roadway while the horse trail continues on to ford Dry Branch. At 1.7 miles, the trail turns left off the roadway to a bridge crossing of Dry Branch. You'll also see that the trail continues straight up the roadway, but it soon swings left to the bridge crossing, so just turn left here at this junction.

On the other side, you'll pass through bottomlands and ascend to an old roadway at 1.8 miles and bear left. You'll cross two footbridges over small streams and reach a junction with the No Business Trail at 2.0 miles. Now the Dry Branch Trail and the No Business Trail coincide along the old roadway paralleling No Business Creek.

You'll pass an old roadway up to the right. At 2.1 miles watch for a row of rocks on the right that may have been foundations for a house. After, a stream runs under the road. Watch for the foundation pillars of the old boarding house down to your left with the massive bluffs of Burke Knob on the other side of the gorge. Where another stream passes under the road, you'll see stacked rocks up to the right that seem to have formed a dam on the stream, but there are so many spaces between the rocks, they do not hold back any water.

At 2.2 miles, you'll reach a junction with the John Muir Trail coming in from the left where the Dry Branch Trail ends. The JMT and the No Business Trail continue straight up the old road.

53 Miller Branch Trail ∩

2.1 miles one-way
Moderate
Elevation loss: 640 ft.
Cautions: Steep descent
Connections: Kentucky Trail ⚎, Difficulty Creek Trail ∩,
No Business Trail ∩

Attractions: This trail provides access to No Business Creek.

Trailhead: Follow the directions in Trail #52 from the Peters Mountain Trailhead to the junction with the Burkes Branch Trail at 3.6 miles. Continue straight to where the Kentucky Trail turns left off the Difficulty Creek Trail at 4.0 miles. Again continue straight to another junction at 4.1 miles with a dirt road to the right that is the Miller Branch Trail. At this writing, the junction has not yet been signed or blazed; you'll just have to watch for the turn. The proposed Difficulty Creek Trail will continue straight from this junction to eventually ford Difficulty Creek and head upriver to connect with the proposed Cat Ridge Trail.

Description: After you make the right turn onto the muddy side road that is the Miller Branch Trail, you'll very soon reach a junction with a wider road and bear left. At 0.4 mile, the road crosses the state line into Tennessee. Then stay straight past a side road on the left; this is the likely route for the proposed Abre Branch Bike Trail, which will head toward Difficulty Creek.

At 0.6 mile, begin a descent into the No Business Creek Gorge. A bar across the road blocks vehicle access. At 0.8 mile, a fork to the right has become overgrown; stay left. As the road curves right, it leads into a steeper descent. At 1.0 mile, you'll descend a steep bank with mud and bare sandstone. The trail soon curves left to cross a small stream. You'll cross the stream again at 1.5 miles and curve left down the cove of Miller Branch. You'll bottom out and reach a junction at 2.1 miles with the No Business Trail that runs along the north side of No Business Creek.

54 No Business Trail ∩

3.1 miles one-way
Easy
Elevation gain: 80 ft.
Cautions: Creek fords, mudholes, multiple-use
with hikers on the John Muir Trail
Connections: Big Island Loop ∩, Miller Branch Trail ∩, Big
Branch Trail ∩, Burkes Branch Trail 🏇, Dry Branch Trail 🏇,
John Muir Trail 🏇, Stoopin Oak Trail ∩,
Longfield Branch Trail ∩

Attractions: This mostly level trail traverses the old community of No Business and serves to connect several trails.

Trailhead: Since this is a connector trail, you must ride other trails to get to it. We describe the trail from the Big South Fork headed west. To get to this east end of the trail you can ride the Miller Branch Trail out of the Peters Mountain Trailhead (Trail #53) or ford the river from the Big Island Loop (Trail #57) or ride the Parch Corn and Big Branch Trails north from the Station Camp Creek and Watson Cemetery Trails (Trail #40).

Description: The No Business Trail begins at the mouth of No Business Creek where it joins the Big South Fork River. You'll see Big Island in the middle of the river; at low water you can ford across to the island and then on across to connect with the Big Island Loop on the east side of the river.

Headed west from the river on the No Business Trail, you'll follow an old roadway that stays on the north side of No Business Creek. You'll first ride over a low ridge and then traverse bottomlands along the creek. At 0.3 mile, you'll reach a junction with the Miller Branch Trail up to the right. Soon after, ford Miller Branch.

At 0.4 mile, the trail drops off to the left as a roadway continues straight. Soon after, watch for a rock wall up to the right that surrounds a collapsed barn and the foundations of a house with the base of a chimney still standing. The No Business

Community of subsistence farms thrived along the creek in the late 1800s and early 1900s.

You'll cross a couple of small streams and then reach a junction at 0.6 mile with a road down to the left. This is the Big Branch Trail that fords No Business Creek and then follows an old road south toward Parch Corn Creek.

Continue up the No Business Trail. As you ascend over a low ridge, you'll see the rock bluffs of Burke Knob across the gorge. Descending from the ridge, you'll cross a couple of small streambeds and reach a junction at 0.9 mile with the foundations of a house on your left. The road straight ahead that is blocked by posts is the Burkes Branch Trail. The No Business Trail turns left here. You'll ford Burkes Branch and continue up the road paralleling No Business Creek.

At 1.1 miles, the trail turns left at a junction with a road straight ahead that is part of the Dry Branch Trail. After making the left turn, you'll ford Dry Branch at 1.2 miles and continue up the road. Crossing a couple of small streams that run across the trail in wet weather, you'll reach a junction at 1.6 miles where the Dry Branch Trail comes in from the right and joins the No Business Trail.

At 1.8 miles, you'll reach a junction with the John Muir Trail coming in from the left. The Dry Branch Trail ends here and now the No Business and John Muir Trails continue up the old road. This was a populated section of the No Business Community; watch for picket fences and stone foundations and rows of rock. At 2.6 miles, watch for the shell of an old truck where a side stream crosses under slabs of rock in the road and tumbled-down log barns rest in the overgrown field to the left. Soon after, you'll pass the Stoopin Oak Trail that leads up to the right. At 2.7 miles, you'll ford Tacket Creek. At 3.0 miles, the John Muir Trail turns off right while the No Business Trail continues straight.

Then at 3.1 miles, the trail ends at a junction with the Longfield Branch Trail that fords No Business Creek to the left. You'll see straight ahead that the old roadbed continues straight, although at this writing it's overgrown. That route will eventually be an extension of the Longfield Branch Loop.

Picket fences at No Business

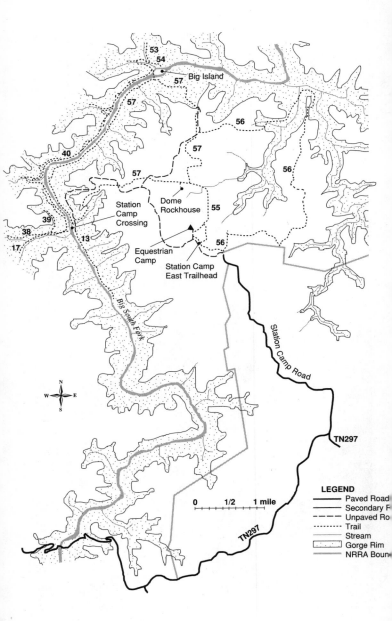

Map 8. Station Camp East
154

55 Dome Rockhouse Trail ∩

1.6 miles one-way
(Dome Rockhouse 2.1 miles one-way)
Moderate
Elevation change: 200 ft.
Cautions: Creek ford
Connections: Pilot/Wines Loop ∩, Big Island Loop ∩

Attractions: This pleasant walk or ride gives access to the Big Island Loop and the rare Dome Rockhouse and is part of the Pilot/Wines Loop.

Trailhead: Outside the park on the east, where TN297 makes a right-angle turn at the Terry and Terry Store, take the Station Camp Road west toward the river. The paved road becomes gravel at 3.7 miles, but it will be paved all the way at some time. Just before entering the park, you'll pass a right turn to the Big South Fork Station Camp Wilderness Resort, which has cabins and stables for overnight stays. You'll cross the boundary into the park at 4.1 miles. At 4.5 miles, turn in the Station Camp East Trailhead on the right. The trail begins at the far west end of the parking area. This trail may also be accessed from the new equestrian camp just down the road on the right. The trail begins to the right just before the gate into the campground; there's also a short trail to the right connecting the camp with the trailhead.

Description: As you head straight into the woods; you'll see the Pilot/Wines Loop to the right. You'll dip through a couple of low wet areas and at 0.7 mile pass through posts to a junction. To the left is the 0.6-mile trail to the equestrian camp.

Turn right. At 1.0 mile you'll cross a bridge over a drainage. The trail descends to a ford of Indian Rock Branch at 1.3 miles. You'll then cross a bridge over a side drainage. The trail then climbs, switchbacks left, and reaches a trail junction at 1.6 miles with the Big Island Loop. Turn left at this junction to reach the Dome Rockhouse at 2.1 miles. See Trail #57 for details.

5️⃣6️⃣ Pilot/Wines Loop ∩

12.0 miles
(Pilot Rock 5.7 miles one-way)
Moderate
Elevation change: 660 ft.
Cautions: Creek fords
Connections: Big Island Loop ∩, Dome Rockhouse Trail ∩

Attractions: This horse trail takes you out to Pilot Rock and the Williams Creek area.

Trailhead: Follow the directions in Trail #55 to the Station Camp East Trailhead on Station Camp Road. The trail begins at the far west end of the parking area.

Description: You'll see the Dome Rockhouse Trail heading straight into the woods, which will be your return on the loop. Turn down right to follow the Pilot/Wines Loop counter-clockwise. You'll circle below the parking area and head east, paralleling Station Camp Road. The trail curves in and out around the heads of coves and at 0.8 mile ascends to a junction with the old Pilot Rock Ridge Road. To the right, you can reach Station Camp Road in 100 yards.

Turn left on Pilot Rock Ridge Road. The road curves right where a side road leads off left. Stay with the main road as side tracks lead off right and left. You'll reach a fork at 1.1 miles; the right fork leads to a gate and private property, so stay left. At 1.4 miles, the trail turns right while a side road continues straight. You'll descend curving left to a ford of a branch of Grassy Fork at 1.5 miles. The road ascends from here to an intersection of roads at 1.9 miles; stay straight. You'll soon make a sharp left and wind down into a cove.

At 3.5 miles, the trail intersects with an old roadway. At this junction, turn left and follow the old road out along Pilot Rock Ridge.

The trail ascends to the top of a knoll at 4.4 miles and curves right. You'll then turn down left to cross a saddle in the ridge.
156

With leaves off the trees, you can see the rock bluffs of Williams Creek Gorge to the right. The trail crosses another saddle and ascends to the top of a knoll at 5.1 miles; bear right again. Soon you'll make a steep descent and then a second descent that switchbacks left and right into a cove with rock bluffs. You'll eventually ascend back to the ridgeline and continue out the narrow ridge to where the trail turns off right at 5.7 miles. At this turn, you can walk straight ahead on a path that takes you 100 yards to Pilot Rock, a massive 100-foot block of stone standing on the point of the ridge.

Making the right turn off the ridge, you'll descend steeply to curve left and circle below Pilot Rock. At 6.4 miles, the trail forks; at this writing the left deadends in a few yards, but this is probably where a proposed trail will complete a loop around Pilot Rock. Stay straight to continue a steep descent to the edge of Grassy Fork at 6.5 miles and a junction. To the right the trail leads 0.1 mile to the confluence of Grassy Fork with Williams Creek. When more trails are constructed, you'll access the Williams Creek Trail to the right.

Back at the junction, turn left to continue on the Pilot/Wines Loop. At 6.6 miles, you'll ford Grassy Fork and make a steep ascent with a switchback right, following the old Wines Road that winds through the bend in the road. You'll level off and reach a junction with an old roadway at 6.9 miles. Turn left to cross a small stream and begin another steep ascent, reaching the top of the plateau at 7.6 miles. Continue a gradual ascent to finally level off and pass a no-vehicle sign and emerge on the Big Island Road at 8.6 miles.

Turn left on the road and at 8.8 miles you'll reach the junction with the Big Island Loop crossing the road. Turn left to head back toward Station Camp East. The trail soon crosses the end of an old roadway. At 10.4 miles you'll reach a junction with the Big Island Loop to the right; turn left on the Dome Rockhouse Trail and follow it back to the Station Camp East Trailhead at 12.0 miles, fording Indian Rock Branch along the way.

🗗7 Big Island Loop ∩

11.0 miles
Elevation change: 620 ft.
Moderate
Cautions: Steep sections, small stream crossings, mudholes
Connections: River Trail East ∩, John Muir Trail 🐎 and
Station Camp Creek and Parch Corn Trails ∩ with a ford of
the river, Pilot/Wines Loop ∩, Dome Rockhouse Trail ∩, No
Business and Big Branch Trails ∩ with a ford of the river

Attractions: This horse trail swings by Big Island where you
can ford to the No Business Creek area.

Trailhead: Follow the directions in Trail #55 to the Station Camp
East Trailhead. Continue down the Station Camp Road, passing
the equestrian camp on the right, where you should begin this
ride if you have a horse trailer; a trail to the right at the gate leads
to the Dome Rockhouse Trail that connects with the Big Island
Loop. Hikers and mountain bikers can continue down the Station
Camp Road. At 2.1 miles, the Big Island Loop crosses the road.
But the best place to start the loop is down at the river, so con-
tinue down the gravel road. At 2.6 miles, you'll pass the Chimney
Rocks on the left, two pillars of stone. At 3.6 miles you'll reach
Station Camp Crossing and a parking area at the end of the road.

Description: At the south end of the parking area, you'll find
the end of the River Trail East that heads toward Angel Falls. To
walk or ride the Big Island Loop, head back up the road from
the parking area. You'll see the river access for the Station Camp
Crossing on your left. You can ford the river here at low water
to reach the John Muir, Station Camp Creek, and Parch Corn
Trails on the other side. Ford only at low water.

Farther up the road, you'll see on your left the end of the
Big Island Loop. We describe the loop counterclockwise; so continue up the road 0.1 mile to where the trail takes a sharp right
off the road. The trail follows an old roadbed until at 0.2 mile
the trail turns up to the left, following another old road. You'll
158

Station Camp Crossing

see rock outcrops on the left, and below on the right Slavens Branch flows down to the river, passing under the road just before the parking area.

At 0.5 mile, you'll ascend to a junction with another old roadbed and turn left. The trail soon curves right with the river now on your left. You'll continue to curve right up a hollow. The trail then curves left through the head of the hollow and into a long ascent. You'll top the ridge and descend through another hollow. As the trail ascends again, stay with the main roadbed as side roads lead off. At 1.5 miles, you'll reach the back of the Slavens Cemetery, which is near the Chimney Rocks.

The trail swings around the cemetery and then curves right to begin ascending again. The trail heads up a drainage steeply to the road at 1.8 miles. Cross the road to the right and reenter the woods. You'll descend into a cove. The trail crosses a bridge over a wet area and at 2.1 miles skirts an overhang where a trickle of water forms a small waterfall. You'll then ascend with a couple of switchbacks to cross an old road and then the graveled Big Island Road off Station Camp Road at 2.6 miles. The trail then descends, following a small streambed on the left.

At 3.0 miles, you'll reach a junction with a 0.1-mile side trail to the right that leads to the Dome Rockhouse. After reaching a hitching area near the end of this side path, continue on foot to the right to reach the rock shelter. The entrance opens to a recessed room where, once your eyes adjust to the dark, you'll see the large hemispherical ceiling.

Back at the main trail, continue north. At 3.5 miles the trail ascends to a junction with the Dome Rockhouse Trail to the right; this is where those riding from the equestrian camp or the Station Camp East Trailhead will access the loop. Continue north at this junction on the Big Island Loop.

The trail follows an old roadbed across the plateau surface headed back toward the Big South Fork. At 4.7 miles, the trail ascends to cross the end of an old road. At 4.9 miles, you'll ascend to recross the graveled Big Island Road. This is where the Pilot/Wines Loop, coming down the road, turns south on the Big Island Loop. At 5.8 miles the trail comes out to the road again where you'll turn left around a gate to descend steeply toward the river. You'll cross a small creek and reach a junction at 7.0

miles in the floodplain of the river. To get to the Big Island Crossing, you would follow the small stream down to the right to the river. Do not attempt a ford of the river except at low water; if you cannot see the bottom, you should probably not try it. On the other side, you can connect with the Big Branch Trail and the No Business Trail. Both sides of the river can be very muddy.

The Big Island Loop now continues south along the Big South Fork, following an old roadbed upstream; you'll probably encounter debris left from floodwaters. Along the way, you'll cross several small streams on stepping stones. At 7.3 miles, notice up to the left the remains of an old cabin that burned.

At 7.8 miles, the trail turns up to a spacious cabin that has been maintained as a backcountry camp. The cabin sits on a knoll below a rock bluff where Cold Springs Branch spills down the hillside in a small waterfall. In spring the slopes above the creek are covered in wildflowers.

From the cabin, descend back down to the trail and continue on the old roadbed, crossing Cold Springs Branch. If there has been rain recently, you'll find the old roadbed is pocked with mudholes that you must negotiate. Some pools have been left by receding floodwaters. Here along the river, you'll see many wildflowers in spring, including occasional large patches of bluebells.

At 8.5 miles, you'll see an old car turned upside down. Then at 9.0 miles, you'll begin to see on your left piles of moss-covered stone and then occasional rock walls that mark an area that was once populated with a farming community. Staying along the river, you'll return to Station Camp Crossing at 11.0 miles.

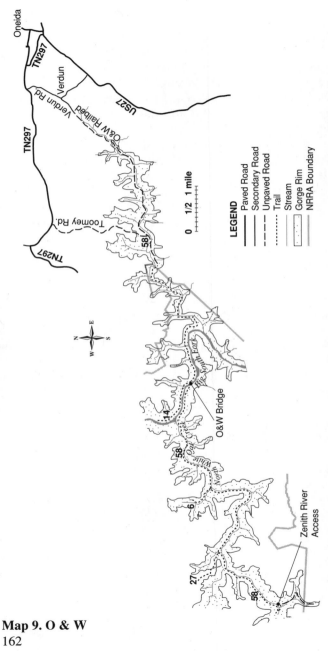

Map 9. O & W

162

🚲🚲 **O&W Railbed** ∩ 🚲

12.4 miles one-way
Moderate
Elevation change: 300 ft.
Cautions: Creek fords, mudholes
Connections: John Muir Trail 👫, Coyle Branch Trail ∩,
Gernt Trail ∩

Attractions: The old railbed runs along Pine Creek down into the Big South Fork Gorge to cross the river on the old O&W Bridge and continue up North White Oak Creek.

Trailhead: The best place to begin the ride along the old O&W Railbed is at the former site of Toomey, one of the camps along the route of the railroad. Headed east from the park on TN297, at 0.6 mile from the corner at the Terry and Terry Store, turn south onto a gravel road. This Toomey Road descends to join the O&W Railbed in 2.5 miles. At the junction you'll find a little room to park. You can also reach the site of Toomey along the railbed. At 1.7 miles west of Oneida on TN297, turn south on Verdun Road. In another 0.6 mile turn right on the railbed, here a paved road. It becomes a graveled road in half a mile as you head down along Pine Creek. You'll cross two bridges over Pine Creek and one over a tributary stream; take care at these bridge crossings. You'll reach the junction with the Toomey Road at 4.2 miles.

Description: The Oneida & Western Railroad operated during the first half of the 1900s, hauling coal and lumber out of the Big South Fork Gorge to Oneida where the material was loaded on the Southern Railway line and shipped out of the region. The O&W extended to Jamestown on the west side of the park. The rail line stopped operating in 1954 and the rails were pulled up. This railbed is now a grand ride for either horses or bikes. At the current time, the route is maintained as a county road down to the river.

From the junction with the Toomey Road, head west along

163

the old railbed. You'll cross a high wooden bridge over Pine Creek; because the planking runs vertically, it's best to walk your bike across so you don't get a tire caught in the space between boards. At 0.5 mile, you'll pass through a narrow section where rock walls encroach on the railbed. At 0.7 mile, you'll cross the boundary into the BSFNRRA.

After penetrating several more narrow sections, the railbed crosses another wooden bridge over the creek at 1.7 miles. You'll then enter a narrows with rock walls on both sides where the railbed has been cut through the rock. At 2.9 miles you'll enter another rock passageway with tall rock walls on both sides. Emerging on the other side, you'll bear right as the railbed now follows the Big South Fork downstream. At 3.0 miles, a road to the left blocked by a gate leads down toward the mouth of Pine Creek.

At 3.9 miles, with the river on your left, you'll see a hollow to the right with layered stone and a wet-weather waterfall. You'll reach the O&W Bridge at 4.5 miles. Stairs on the left lead down to the river. Just before the bridge, you'll see the John Muir Trail on the right coming in from Leatherwood Ford. When the JMT is completed south, it will cross the O&W Bridge and then turn left to ascend Hurricane Ridge.

Walk your bike or horse across the 200-foot bridge, erected 1914-15. On the other side, continue along the railbed as it parallels the river downstream. At 4.8 miles, a cascading stream on the left passes through a culvert under the railbed.

At 5.4 miles, you'll pass through another narrows as the railbed curves left to follow North White Oak Creek upstream. Turn left at 5.8 miles on a rocky path that leads down to the creek; the railbed straight once led to a bridge over the creek. Now you must ford the creek; enter the creek only a low water. You'll regain the railbed on the other side. A side path left at 6.0 miles leads down to the creek. You'll then continue along the railbed with the creek on your left and occasional rock walls on the right. You'll encounter an occasional long mudhole. At 8.0 miles, you'll reach a junction with the Coyle Branch Trail that follows the old Coyle Branch Road up to the right; the road is blocked by posts. Continue straight to a ford of Coyle Branch.

Heading down along Coyle Branch, you'll see there was

once a rail bridge over the creek. You'll then curve right to continue up North White Oak Creek. At 9.4 miles, you'll cross a washed out area in the railbed. A side road to the left at 9.9 miles leads down to a campsite and swimming hole in the creek.

You'll turn up to ford Groom Branch at 10.5 miles and then turn back down; there was once a rail bridge over this side creek also. At 10.7 miles, you'll reach a junction with the Gernt Trail that follows the old Gernt Road up to the right; the road is blocked by posts.

Continue on the old railbed. At 10.9 miles, you'll pass a beautiful campsite on the left with a huge block of stone sitting beside the creek. Soon after, you'll reach a fork where the old railbed turns down to the left. The road straight heads up the Laurel Fork of North White Oak Creek for a couple of miles.

Head down the left fork, you'll see on your left old bridge supports on both sides where the rail line crossed the creek. Just downstream to the left, Laurel Fork joins North White Oak Creek. You must ford Laurel Fork, only at low water, and then turn up left to regain the railbed.

Continue on the railbed. At 12.4 miles, you'll reach a turn down to the left. The railbed continues on but eventually becomes overgrown. The left turn takes you down to a ford of North White Oak Creek to the Zenith River Access on the other side.

Cross if you intend to emerge at the Zenith area. On the other side, bear left downstream along the creek; a road to the right leads to a campsite on a side creek. Stay with the road, and at 12.7 miles, ford Camp Branch above where it joins North White Oak Creek. On the other side, you'll connect with the Zenith Road. Zenith was another of the loading stations along the O&W; some old foundations lie off to your left. To the left, this road fords North White Oak Creek.

Turn right on Zenith Road and make a steep climb out of the North White Oak Creek Gorge. At 14.5 miles, after crossing Camp Branch on a bridge and following the south fork of the branch upstream, you'll emerge on the paved Mt. Helen Road. To the right it's 5.5 miles out to TN52, 7.1 miles west of Rugby; or your could turn left to reach the Honey Creek area of the park in 5 miles and the Burnt Mill Bridge River Access beyond.

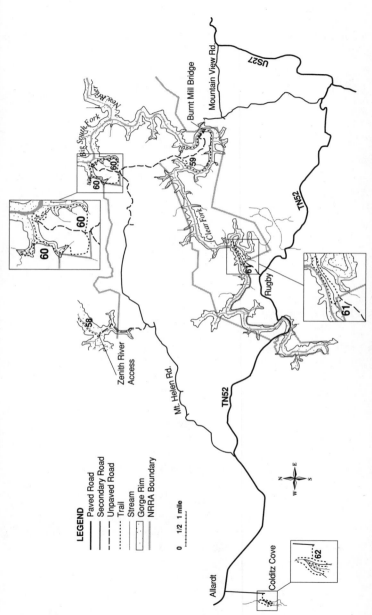

Map 10. Burnt Mill Bridge/Rugby/Colditz Cove
166

59 Burnt Mill Bridge Loop 🏃🏃

3.6 miles
Moderate
Elevation change: 200 ft.
Cautions: Stairs
Connections: John Muir Trail segment 🏃🏃

Attractions: This loop parallels the Clear Fork River with good wading pools and wildflowers in spring.

Trailhead: On US27, 10 miles south of Oneida and 4.6 miles north of Elgin, turn west on Mountain View Road to head west toward the Burnt Mill Bridge River Access. At 1.6 miles, turn right, then left, and at 3.8 miles at a four-way intersection, turn right again on a small side road. (You can also reach this point if you are coming from the west on TN52; a half mile west of Elgin turn north and go 3.3 miles to the four-way intersection and keep straight ahead.) Bear left in another half mile on a gravel road, and then in another 0.4 mile, you'll cross Burnt Mill Ford Bridge to the west side of the Clear Fork River. Parking is on the left. Do not drive across this old bridge in a large vehicle, such as a bus or a large RV. You can also get to this trailhead from the west to avoid the bridge crossing by turning north on the Mt. Helen Road off TN52 7.1 miles west of Rugby; at 5 miles along this road stay left at a fork; the road becomes gravel at 8 miles and you'll pass the turnoff on the left for Honey Creek at 10 miles and then reach the Burnt Mill Ford Bridge at 14 miles. The ford that people used before the bridge was built got its name from the burning of a nearby grist mill on the river's east side.

Description: Walk across the road from trailhead parking to where the trail leads down steps into the woods to parallel Clear Fork downstream. Watch for side paths that give you access to the river. The cool forest and places for taking a dip in the river make this a trail to hike in the summer. Spring and early summer, wildflowers litter the forest floor.

You'll soon pick up a rock wall on your left. The trail cross-

167

Burnt Mill Ford Bridge
168

es two footbridges over wet areas. You'll climb slightly and then drop back to the edge of the river by a wooden stairway at 0.2 mile. The trail then passes under a low overhang. Then at 0.4 mile, you'll turn up a side stream to climb away from the river. You'll cross the creekbed on three footbridges as you continue up this side drainage. The trail then joins an old road.

The trail turns left off the road but then rejoins it soon after to continue up the road. At 0.7 mile, you'll reach the junction with a lower section of the John Muir Trail. If you hike this trail to the right, beware that it is blazed for only the first half mile and eventually deadends in a maze of old roads; don't get lost. Plans call for the JMT to be constructed south from the O&W Bridge to connect with this section of trail.

Bear left to continue the loop, and soon you'll cross the road up from Burnt Mill Bridge. Back into the woods, you'll cross a footbridge over a small drainage at 1.0 mile and soon begin a descent back toward the Clear Fork. The trail switchbacks right and left and drops along a ravine with rock walls up to the right to reach the river at 1.7 miles. Bear left downstream.

Again the river will be on your right as you follow a rock bluff on your left. Watch for several places to walk out on rocks that stand at the river's edge and places where you can easily go wading. You'll also pass several campsites along the way.

At 2.2 miles, the trail passes under a tall overhang. You'll enter a large campsite with easy access to wading in the creek at 2.3 miles. You'll cross a drainage and join an old roadway along the creek at 2.6 miles. The road soon forks; stay to the right along the creek. After passing under another overhang, the old road turns down toward the river while the trail ascends; you'll cross another old roadway down to the river at 3.2 miles. The trail soon after rejoins the old road.

At 3.4 miles, a path to the right leads down to the river; stay left and then veer right off the old roadway. You'll cross a footbridge over a drainage and reach the end of the parking area at the trailhead and close the loop at 3.6 miles.

You can take one last dip under the Burnt Mill Ford Bridge; this is a popular swimming hole and also a favored put-in for river runners.

⑥⓪ Honey Creek Loop 🏃🏃

5.2 miles
Difficult
Elevation change: 460 ft.
Cautions: Stream crossings impassable in high water,
caged ladders, boulder passages, steep slopes
Connections: Honey Creek Overlook Trail 🏃🏃

Attractions: This fascinating loop has rock shelters, gorge overlooks, waterfalls, streams, boulder passages.

Trailhead: Follow the directions in Trail #59 to the Burnt Mill Ford Bridge and continue up the road. At 3.4 miles take a right fork 0.1 mile to a wide area where you can park on the left. The trail begins just ahead on the right side of the road. This gravel road continues 0.8 mile to the Honey Creek Overlook of the Big South Fork. Trail #59 also gives directions from the west.

Description: The trail climbs a few steps from the road and swings left to ascend the hill through a pine woods. Across the top of the ridge, you'll join an old road to the right at 0.2 mile. The trail curves away from the road to the right and then descends to cross it at 0.4 mile and begin a steep descent.

You'll descend to a small stream at 0.6 mile and cross a footbridge over a tributary at 0.9 mile. As the stream drops more steeply into a hemlock and rhododendron cove, the trail curves left up steps to swing by a rock wall at 1.1 miles. The curious swirls in the rock are iron deposits that erode more slowly than the encasing stone. The trail then switchbacks right to descend back to creek level at a small waterfall.

At 1.2 miles, the trail turns left up the slope to ascend over a low rock overhang. Descending, you'll reach the bottom of 10-foot Moonshine Falls. The trail crosses the stream at the foot of the waterfall and turns downstream to cross again at 1.3 miles. You'll descend through switchbacks, a narrow wooden bridge, and a slippery slope back to the main creek. Turn downstream.

The trail follows a massive rock wall to a large beech tree.

Turn left up the steep slope to a junction at 1.4 miles. The Honey Creek Overlook Trail to the left leads up ladders, switchbacks, and steps to the top of the bluff, where it then swings right along the rim, crossing a small creek, to the overlook; on the other side, the trail then descends through ladders and steps to return to the main trail. Because you can now drive to the overlook, we recommend staying on the trail below.

You'll walk along the rock bluff, which leans over the trail. The roar from the river echoes off the wall. Beyond is Hideout Falls, a tall, slender waterfall created by the small stream you'd cross on the overlook trail. You'll reach the junction with the other end of the overlook trail at 1.6 miles. Turn right down a steep slope and curve left to walk above the river.

The trail then curves left up the Honey Creek drainage. At 1.9 miles, curve right and descend steeply to Honey Creek. Turn left along the creek. Soon you must bear right through boulders into the creekbed. Cross the top of a boulder and curve left to get out of the creek. At 2.2 miles, the trail crosses the creek and then turns downstream to a low rock overhang, where the trail turns right to go around and head up the slope. The trail ascends to pass a large boulder with a hemlock growing on it and a good campsite.

The trail now works its way into the drainage for the North Fork of Honey Creek. Through a rock squeeze; turn left. At 2.3 miles, you'll reach the junction with the Indian Rockhouse Loop to the right. Straight and curving up the slope to the left is a 100-foot shortcut to the main trail. If you have had trouble crossing the creek already, the side loop is certainly impassable and you should take this shortcut. But in times of low water, turn right.

You'll soon reach the North Fork. You must enter the creek and make your way upstream the best you can, occasionally climbing over boulders. Along the way, you'll enter a narrow gorge. At 2.4 miles, Indian Rockhouse opens in the bluff on the left. You'll then head down the right side of the creek in a rhododendron thicket, curve left to cross the creek, and pass another rock shelter. The trail then reenters the stream. At 2.5 miles head up the slope to the left. The trail switchbacks a couple of times and passes a low, rock shelter and then switches left above the rock wall. You'll parallel the cliff through a pine wood.

The trail reaches a junction at 2.8 miles with the other end of the shortcut. Stay straight. You'll switchback in a descent to Boulder House Falls and a creek ford at 3.1 miles. The trail then turns right to pass through a rock maze and come out above the waterfall. The trail curves left to cross the creek and climb steeply up the slope. At 3.2 miles you'll pass a rock shelter and reach a junction with a right side trail to Tree-Top Rock; it's 100 feet to the large block of stone with a hemlock growing on top.

The main trail curves left and descends steeply to a stream; to the right is a small half-waterfall, half-cascade. Downstream to the left, you'll cross the creek and climb steeply up the opposite slope; watch for a right turn at 3.3 miles. After passing under an overhang, the trail turns right down stone steps to another creek crossing above the small waterfall. Bear left upstream to enter a narrow gorge.

The trail turns away from the creek and ascends the slope. At the top, you'll walk onto an expanse of bare rock with patches of reindeer moss at 3.5 miles. Turn left and reenter the woods. The trail curves right to head upstream high above Honey Creek. At 3.6 miles, you'll be above Honey Creek Falls.

Curve down left to a creek crossing on a footbridge at 3.7 miles. Then walk downstream on the other side. After passing the top of the falls again, the trail curves away from the creek to a left side trail to the waterfall at 3.9 miles. Taking this side trail, you'll scramble through the drainage of a small tributary 50 yards to a view of 20-foot Honey Creek Falls plunging into a deep green pool embedded in a rock grotto.

Continue up the main trail, which crosses the small tributary. You'll pass a large pool on the right. Continue ascending. The trail then turns right to cross the stream at 4.0 miles; this turn is easy to miss because there is also a path that continues straight. The trail swings right to pass above the pool.

You'll ascend the ridge, cross an old road, and descend into the drainage for another tributary of Honey Creek. At 4.4 miles, turn left and walk upstream through thickets of rhododendron and laurel. At 4.6 miles the trail ascends away from the creek, crosses two branches of an old road, and continues to gradually ascend. You'll cross a stream twice and head up the slope to cross an old road and return to the trailhead at 5.2 miles.

Boulder House Falls

⑥1 Gentlemen's Swimming Hole/ Meeting of the Waters Loop 🚶🚶

2.0 miles
(Swimming Hole 0.4 mile one-way)
Moderate
Elevation change: 240 ft.
Cautions: Creek crossings, rocky and steep in places,
mudholes on return portion
Connections: None

Attractions: Rugby is an important historic attraction of the region. On your visit, you can walk this trail into the BSFNRRA to the swimming hole on the Clear Fork River and to the confluence of White Oak Creek.

Trailhead: Historic Rugby, founded in 1880, is located 7 miles west of Elgin and 18 miles east of Jamestown on TN52. There's lodging at Newbury House and Pioneer Cottage and at nearby Clear Fork Farm and Grey Gables Bed and Breakfasts. West of the center of the community, turn north on the Donnington Road, a gravel road that leads to the Laurel Dale Cemetery. Along this road and along the trail, numbered posts mark points of interest; brochures can be had at the Rugby visitor center or at the Bandy Creek Visitor Center. At the end of the road, you'll find the cemetery and, to the left, parking for the Rugby Trailhead.

Description: The last English colony in the U.S., Rugby was founded by English writer Thomas Hughes as a home for second sons of English gentry. When Hughes visited the colony in 1880, he awoke the first morning to the sounds of young men gathering. "In a few minutes," he wrote, "several appeared in flannel shirts and trousers, bound for one of the two rivers which run close by. . . . They had heard of a pool 10 feet deep . . . and a most delicious place it is, surrounded by great rocks, lying in a copse of rhododendrons, azaleas, and magnolias." The pool the young men were bound for was the Gentlemen's Swimming

Christ Church at Rugby

Hole.

Follow the trail from the cemetery. The path descends through a mixed hardwood and pine forest. You'll continue to see numbered posts corresponding with the brochure that interprets the surrounding forest. The trail descends to cross into the BSFNRRA, winding down to a creek crossing at 0.2 mile where you'll be able to step across. The trail then turns right and descends several stone steps while following the creek as it cascades down into a cove of rhododendron and hemlock.

The main trail curves to the right while still descending. The creek drops over a ledge in a two-step waterfall. You'll step over the creek below this waterfall. The trail then curves around a rock bluff. At 0.4 mile, you'll reach a junction with a side trail that leads down to the Gentlemen's Swimming Hole. Straight ahead, the trail leads on to the Meeting of the Waters.

The side path is a short walk down to the shore of the river and the swimming hole. To the right, a long rock juts into the water; it's easy to picture the young men of Rugby taking a flying leap into the river from the end of the rock. Take care if you go swimming; search the water for rocks before diving.

On the main trail, continue north through thick rhododendron. The trail for the next mile travels along the strip of land between the rock bluff to your right and the river's edge on the left, occasionally nearing the rock wall. You'll see rock overhangs in the wall and huge blocks of stone that have fallen into the river. In wet weather, water drips from the overhangs and runs down the rock wall. In winter watch for falling icicles.

At 1.1 miles, you'll reach the confluence of White Oak Creek with the Clear Fork River. The trail curves right and drops to bare rock at the edge of White Oak Creek with the "Meeting of the Waters" just to the left. You'll then ascend, steeply in places with steps; watch for ice in winter. As you near the top of the White Oak Creek Gorge, the forest opens at a junction with an old road. Turn right and continue ascending to a junction with another road at 1.2 miles. Turn right again. Walking along the road, you'll encounter several mudholes if it has rained recently and at 1.6 miles pass tanks on the right with a natural-gas pipe sticking out of the ground. The road returns to the trailhead at 2.0 miles.

⑥② **Colditz Cove Loop** 🏃

1.5 miles
Moderate
Elevation change: 100 ft.
Cautions: Steep descent, boulder passages
Connections: None

Attractions: Colditz Cove is a Tennessee State Natural Area near the southern border of the BSFNRRA. Because this is one of the loveliest spots on the Cumberland Plateau, you should combine this hike with your visit to Rugby. Big Branch drops 60 feet into Colditz Cove to form Northrup Falls.

Trailhead: Colditz Cove is off TN52 11 miles west of Rugby and east of the Allardt town center. Turn south on the Crooked Creek Hunting Lodge Road. In one mile along this road, turn right into the parking area.

Description: Walk around the gate and down an old road. As you walk through scrub forest, you'll probably wonder if this is going to be a waste of time. But as if walking through a door, the forest turns to a lush, green wonderland. Even in winter, the cove is green because of the profusion of hemlocks and rhododendron.

Just before the edge of the cove and a precarious view of the top of Northrup Falls on Big Branch, you'll encounter the loop part of the trail at 0.3 mile. The waterfall is named for a family that once lived here. Turn left to walk the loop clockwise.

The trail passes along the bluff to a good view of the falls. You'll cross a bridge over a small drainage and at 0.5 mile turn right to drop into the cove in a short descent with switchbacks. The trail then doubles back along the base of the rock wall, moving over rocks and ducking behind a small waterfall formed by the stream you crossed above. You'll then enter a long rock shelter that sweeps around to Northrup Falls. You'll need to pass over boulders to the back of the rock shelter to stay on the trail.

The trail passes behind the falls at 0.7 mile; you may get

Northrup Falls
178

wet if there is enough water to kick up a good mist. You'll then pass along the rock wall on the other side with seeps and trickles of water in wet weather; watch for a spout of water coming out of the rock wall after a recent rain. You'll begin the gradual ascent out of the cove, turning right at 0.8 mile, to return to the top of the plateau. The trail then circles back, crossing a bridge over Big Branch, to the beginning of the loop at 1.3 miles. You then must walk the old road back to the parking area at 1.5 miles.

Colditz Cove State Natural Area is practically within the community of Allardt, which was originally a German colony founded about the same time as Rugby. While the English colony was not a great financial success, the Germans who came from Michigan and directly from Germany to settle the town were successful in establishing a good financial base combining farming, lumbering, and coal mining.

The architecture of the town is not as elaborate as that of Rugby, which is probably why Rugby is so much better known. But you can still find here the small white building in the center of town that is the Gernt Office where the descendants of Bruno Gernt, who founded the community along with M. H. Allardt, still manage the family's holdings. The town was named for Allardt, who died just as the settlement began to form. East of the Gernt Office stands the abandoned Colditz Store that operated until 1962. Rudolph and Arnold Colditz donated Colditz Cove to the state of Tennessee. The hiking trail through the natural area was constructed by volunteers with the Cumberland Mountain Chapter of the Tennessee Trails Association.

East from the center of Allardt, off TN52 on a gravel road, you can visit the old Bruno Gernt House, a large gray farmhouse with brick-red trim that is on the National Historic Register. The house is open to the public as a bed & breakfast. This is a favorite place for us; we were married here in 1988.

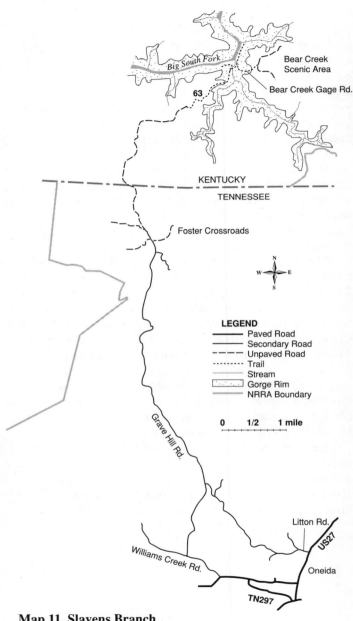

Map 11. Slavens Branch
180

⑥⑬ Huling Branch/
Big Shoals Trails ∩

1.6 miles one-way
Moderate
Elevation loss: 450 ft.
Cautions: Currently unmaintained, steep and rocky
Connections: None for now

Attractions: You'll drop to the mouth of Bear Creek at the river's edge to preview an area where new trails will be located. This is a proposed trail and, until developed, should only be attempted by experienced outdoors people.

Trailhead: To get to the site of the proposed Slavens Branch Trailhead, turn west off US27 on Litton Road in Oneida 0.9 mile north of the junction of US27 and TN297. In 0.2 mile bear left on Grave Hill Road, and then at 0.5 mile keep right to stay on Grave Hill. At 2.1 miles keep left and you'll arrive at Foster Crossroads at 7.4 miles. (Or if you're coming from the park on TN297, at 3.8 miles east of the right turn of TN297 at the Terry and Terry Store, turn north on Williams Creek Road. At 4.5 miles turn right to connect with the Grave Hill Road at 5.9 miles. Turn left another 5 miles to Foster Crossroads.) At the Foster Cross Road Baptist Church, take the far right gravel road 1.0 mile down to cross the Kentucky state line and also the boundary of the BSFNRRA onto Little Bill Slaven Road. At 3.2 miles you'll reach the end of the Slaven Road.

Description: At the end of the road, an old road turns right and drops into the woods; no vehicles allowed beyond this point. There is also the trace of an old road straight that's overgrown. The road you follow to the right will eventually be part of the Huling Branch Loop. Until the trail is cleared, horse riders and mountain bikers will have a difficult time where the trail is overgrown and trees lie across the path.

You'll make a gradual descent along the old roadway, first

headed east and then north. At 0.1 mile, in a section overgrown with briers, keep to the right until you reach the roadbed again and begin a steeper descent. At 0.2 mile, where we had to circle a barrier of down trees when we where last there, notice the forest floor to the right covered in partridge-berry.

At 0.4 mile a rock ledge to the right hangs over the cove created by the Line Fork of Bear Creek below. Along a level section of trail at 0.7 mile, the road swings left around a point with a massive rock bluff up to your left. You'll then make a steep, rocky descent and reach a junction at 1.0 mile with another road to the left; you'll see Bear Creek ahead.

The road left will be the route of the Huling Branch Loop, which will head down the creek to the river and then follow the river upstream and turn up Huling Branch to circle back to the trailhead; if the trail has not yet been cleared, you can still follow this road left for about half a mile. The Line Fork Loop hiking trail is to be constructed to the right at this junction to head upstream along Bear Creek and then up Line Fork to cross the creek twice and then cross its tributary, Slaven Branch, as the trail circles back to the trailhead; it'll be a few years.

Continue straight from this junction to a ford of Bear Creek. Follow the road up the bank on the other side and reach a junction at 1.2 miles with a path down to the left that leads 100 yards to the edge of the Big South Fork at the mouth of Bear Creek.

Just beyond the junction with the path down to the river, you'll connect with the Bear Creek Gaging Station Road; you'll see the concrete tower for the Bear Creek Gage for measuring the river flow. The gravel road leads a half mile steeply up to the Bear Creek Road near a parking area that will be designated the Bear Creek Equestrian Trailhead, 0.3 mile south of parking for the Bear Creek Overlook and the Split Bow Arch Trailhead.

You can continue north from this junction, still following the old road, for a short way. The Gaging Station Road and this route north along the river will become part of the proposed Big Shoals Trail; also a proposed Warbler hiking trail will lead north along the river. You'll pass a gate and then a building that is part of the monitoring station, and at 1.6 miles, reach Salt Branch where the roadway disappears at this writing.

Big South Fork River at Bear Creek

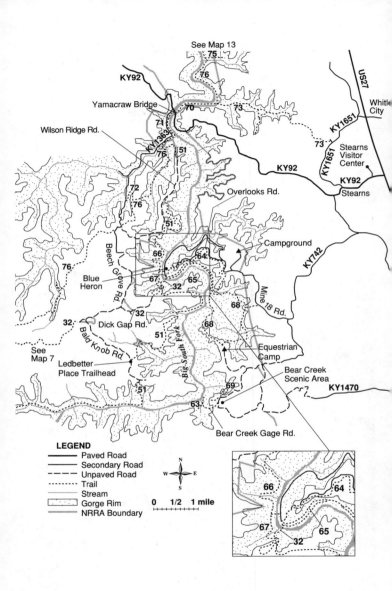

Map 12. Blue Heron/Bear Creek/Yamacraw Bridge
184

⑥4 Blue Heron Loop 🏃🏃

6.6 miles
(Cracks-in-the-Rock 0.6 mile one-way)
(Devils Jump 0.4 mile one-way in reverse direction)
Moderate
Elevation change: 450 ft.
Cautions: Boulder passages, steep stairs
Connections: Kentucky Trail 🏃🏃, Devils Jump and Blue Heron
Overlooks 🏃🏃, Laurel Branch Trail ∩, Long Trail ∩

Attractions: From the historic Blue Heron Mining Community, this trail offers overlooks, rock formations, and river rapids.

Trailhead: North on US27 from Tennessee, or south on US27 in Kentucky, turn west on KY92 toward Stearns. You'll pass a BSFNRRA information center off to the right. In the former company town for the Stearns Coal and Lumber Company, you can pick up the BSF Scenic Railway for a train ride down to Blue Heron and stay overnight at the Big South Fork Motor Lodge or the Marcum-Porter House. To drive to Blue Heron, bear left on KY1651 in Stearns. In 1.1 miles, in Revelo, turn right on KY742. At the left turnoff for the Bear Creek Scenic Area, the road becomes the Mine 18 Road. You'll pass the campground on the right and the Overlooks Road on the left. Once you get to Blue Heron, at 8.2 miles from Revelo, begin the hike near the snack bar at the far end of the parking area; stairs lead up to a walkway.

Description: Blue Heron was a coal mining camp built by the Stearns Company in the early 1900s. The community has been resurrected as a historic exhibit with frame structures showing the locations of the houses and buildings that were gathered around the old tipple, used to separate chunks of coal by size.

From the top of the stairs, turn left up the walkway. You'll pass the tram bridge that leads to the Kentucky Trail on the river's west side. At 0.2 mile the Blue Heron Loop turns right to leave the community. After a couple of ascending switchbacks

Blue Heron Tipple
186

and footbridges, the trail curves up stone steps to Cracks-in-the-Rock at 0.6 mile. You'll find stairs sandwiched between rock monoliths. Over the stairs, turn left to exit. Curve around the rocks and ascend a flight of stairs up a rock crack; turn left.

The trail turns right at 0.7 mile where an unofficial path to the left leads out to a rock shelf offering a view of the Blue Heron tipple and bridge. Climbing gradually from this side path, you'll reach a junction at 0.9 mile with a side trail left that leads up to the Blue Heron Overlook off the Overlooks Road. Keep right. At 1.2 miles, you'll come to the Devils Jump Overlook parking area. Follow the paved path until the trail turns off left.

At 2.0 miles a path leads out to Overlooks Road and additional trail access. You'll occasionally skirt Overlooks Road, and then swing right to parallel Mine 18 Road. Stairs lead up to the road at 3.2 miles. Turn right, staying on this side of the guardrail.

You'll reach a junction with an old road at 3.9 miles. Left it's 100 yards out to the highway across from the road into the campground. Turn right and follow the old road down the ridge. The trail drops through boulders and skirts rock shelves as it descends. Watch your head at a low overhang. You'll reach stairs that drop to a junction with the Laurel Branch Trail at 4.8 miles. Turn right. There's an immediate fork; stay left with the Blue Heron Loop. You'll follow the river north through former coal mine areas. At 5.7 miles you'll rejoin the Laurel Branch Trail on the tramroad. Turn left; you'll soon pass a small waterfall.

At 5.9 miles the trail turns left off the tramroad down steep steps to cross a reclaimed mine area. Descend toward the river and swing right into the woods on the lower side of a settling pond, following an old road. At 6.2 miles, the trail turns left off the road. Soon a side trail leads down to Devils Jump, a rapids in a narrow part of the river. Use caution near the water's edge; boulders can be slick and the currents are strong.

The trail emerges at the Blue Heron area at 6.6 miles. River access leads down to the left for canoes and rafts and for horse riders that ford from the west side after riding the Long Trail; this is also the beginning of the Laurel Branch Trail that turns up right. Walk into the parking area straight ahead. Stairs to the right lead up to the upper level parking where you began the hike.

Cracks-in-the-Rock
188

⑥⑤ Laurel Branch Trail ∩

1.9 miles one-way
Easy
Mostly level
Cautions: Stream ford
Connections: Long Trail ∩, Blue Heron Loop 🐎,
Lee Hollow Loop ∩

Attractions: This pleasant ride along an old tramroad links the Blue Heron Mining Community with the Lee Hollow Loop.

Trailhead: Follow the directions in Trail #64 to the Blue Heron Mining Community and proceed to the far end of the lower parking area. A ramp leads down to the river access and the ford for the Long Trail. The Blue Heron Loop heads straight ahead from the parking area, while the Laurel Branch Trail turns up to the left.

Description: After a short steep climb, you'll reach the grass-covered old tramroad. To the left you'll see a picnic shelter and the snack shop. Turn right. At 0.1 mile, hitching rails stand on the left. At 0.3 mile, another tramroad comes in from the left; this one leads from the upper part of the old mining operations. At 0.5 mile, you'll pass a trail down to the right that leads 100 yards to connect with the Blue Heron Loop. You can walk down the hiking trail to see the Devils Jump Rapids in 0.3 mile.

The trail continues along the old tramroad; you'll see remains of mining operations along the way. At 0.6 mile the horse trail joins the Blue Heron Loop while both use the old tramroad. Then at 0.9 mile the hiking trail turns off to the right. At 1.7 miles, you'll curve left up the cove of Laurel Branch and at 1.8 miles reach another junction with the Blue Heron Loop. Continue straight to a ford of Laurel Branch and bear right up to a junction at 1.9 miles with the Lee Hollow Loop. From here you can ride the loop either way to get to the new horse camp at the Bear Creek Scenic Area. Left along the loop, you can leave the park and reach the Mine 18 Road in 1.3 miles from this junction.

⑥⑥ Old Tramroad 🏃🏃

2.3 miles one-way
Moderate
Elevation gain: 100 ft.
Cautions: Marshy areas, stream crossing, boulder passages
Connections: Kentucky Trail 🏃🏃

Attractions: This trail follows the roadbed of an old electric tram once used to haul coal to the Blue Heron tipple.

Trailhead: Follow the directions in Trail #64 to Blue Heron.

Description: When the Blue Heron tipple was operating, small electric engines pulled tramcars from the west side of the Big South Fork over the high bridge that still spans the river. The trams, open railway cars, were loaded with coal from several mines. The tram bridge is now a footbridge that connects with the Kentucky Trail on the river's west side. Take the bridge across. On the other side, turn right. You'll follow the old tramroad that ran up and down the west side of the river.

At 0.1 mile you'll cross a boardwalk and a bridge to where the trail forks; stay right. At 0.3 mile, upright posts on the left carried the electric lines for the tram system. Switchbacks take you up to a junction with the upper roadbed; turn right. This part of the trail is overgrown in summer and marshy in rainy seasons.

At 1.2 miles, turn right off the road to descend to a crossing of Devils Creek; most times you'll be able to rockhop. The trail then climbs to rejoin the old tramroad. At 1.8 miles, you'll see evidence of mining—pits in the side of the hill to your left, spoil down the slope to your right, coal underfoot. More tram utility poles stand beside the trail. At 2.0 miles the trail curves left as it once more parallels the Big South Fork. Watch for a tiny cinder block building in a mining area. At 2.3 miles, two concrete piers on the right anchored some sort of mining structure. You can turn around to return to Blue Heron; the Kentucky Trail continues north for several more miles.

⑥⑦ Catawba Overlook and Big Spring Falls 🚶🚶

3.6 miles one-way
(Catawba Overlook 1.6 miles one-way)
Moderate
Elevation change: 400 ft.
Cautions: Stream crossings, steep stairs, mudholes, poison ivy
Connections: Kentucky Trail 🚶🚶, Long Trail ∩

Attractions: This trail climbs to a scenic view of the river from Catawba Overlook and reaches a waterfall in Big Spring Hollow.

Trailhead: Follow the directions in Trail #64 to Blue Heron. Cross the river on the tram bridge to west side of the river.

Description: To the right from this end of the tipple bridge, the Kentucky Trail leads along the old tramroad. Turn left from this end of the tipple bridge to walk the Kentucky Trail south. A boardwalk helps you over a marshy area, but you may still have to slog your way through some other parts of the trail if there has been a recent rain. Watch for abandoned tramcars tipped over to the left of the trail. Also watch for a few of the utility posts that still stand beside the tramroad; they held the wires carrying electricity for the tramline.

You'll cross a plank bridge and at 0.2 mile reach a fork in the trail. The left fork has been closed for some years due to slides. This trail continuing along the old tramroad is slated for repair, and once it has been reopened, the two forks will create the Catawba Overlook Loop.

For the time being, take the upper trail to the right from the fork to cross a short footbridge. You'll join an old roadbed and then bear left to Three West Hollow at 0.4 mile. Cross the creek on a footbridge and switchback left. The trail climbs from the creek and crosses a footbridge over a wet-weather stream at 0.5 mile. You'll reach a great rock bluff on your right at 0.6 mile. Watch for wildflowers in spring: purple phacelia, stone crop, vi-

Big Spring Falls
192

olets, foamflower. Continue walking along the rock bluff through a forest of mixed hardwoods, cross another footbridge, and at 1.0 mile climb steep wooden stairs over a rock shelf lined with rhododendron.

You'll cross another footbridge, and at 1.1 miles the trail briefly joins a horse trail. This section of the Long Trail, will be called the "Dick Gap Trail." To your left the horse trail descends a steep rocky slope to cross the lower part of the Catawba Overlook Loop and reach the river ford across to Blue Heron. Just beyond this junction, the hiking trail turns left off the horse trail; you can follow the horse trail up to the right for 0.2 mile to reach the end the Dick Gap Road and walk 0.2 mile out to the Dick Gap Overlook of Blue Heron.

Turning left on the hiking trail, you'll cross a footbridge to head toward the bluff's edge at 1.6 miles and the Catawba Overlook, named for the Catawba rhododendron that blooms rose-purple in May. A short side trail takes you down to your left to a point of rock looking out over the river gorge. To the left the tram bridge spans the river, and below to the right, Devils Jump roils the water's surface.

From Catawba Overlook, follow the trail south; in late summer the path becomes a little overgrown. In places it's thick with poison ivy. The trail drops into a cove. At 1.9 miles, you'll cross a stream on a boardwalk. You'll ascend from the stream and join an old roadbed, but then bear left off the road.

At 2.1 miles, you'll use a set of wooden stairs to climb over a hemlock lying across the trail. Soon after, you'll descend a set of stairs down a bluff and bear left to join an old road once more that leads to Dick Gap Falls at 2.3 miles. The slender waterfall is off the trail to the left.

The trail bears right past the falls, and at 2.4 miles you'll join an old roadbed and switchback left. You'll hear a small stream to the right and then descend stone steps to cross the stream. You'll see to the left where this side stream joins the stream that runs from Dick Gap Falls.

As you continue down the old roadbed, the main stream cascades down a small gorge. You'll descend to a junction at 2.6 miles with the old tramroad where the bottom part of the Catawba Overlook Loop will connect. Turn right on the tramroad along the Big South Fork.

As the trail turns up a side gorge watch for a slag slope at 3.2 miles and then a vent hole for a mine up to your right. At 3.3 miles, the trail crosses Big Spring Creek; the last time we hiked this trail, the bridge had collapsed. Some old foundations lie on the left on the far side of the creek. You'll switchback left and right and, at 3.4 miles, left again where a side trail to the right leads 0.2 mile to Big Spring Falls. You'll first ascend a few stone steps and later cross a boardwalk over a marshy area at the dripline of a rock overhang; watch out for sprinkling water and, in winter, falling icicles. The path then crosses a small stream and ascends stone steps on its way to the falls. The 60-foot waterfall spills halfway down to splash on a rock ledge before making its second drop into a pool at the base.

The Kentucky Trail continues southwest to the Ledbetter Place Trailhead in another 3.6 miles. To reach this trailhead, take KY92 west from Stearns to the Yamacraw Bridge over the Big South Fork. On the west side of the river, turn south on KY1363. The road soon curves right and follows Rock Creek upstream. At 2.3 miles from KY92, turn left on the graveled Beech Grove/ Devils Creek Road that crosses Rock Creek on a concrete bridge. The road soon becomes paved again. At 3.7 miles, the Sheltowee Trace joins the road from the left as you pass Wilson Ridge Road; the Kentucky Trail emerges on that road 2.2 miles to the left. The Sheltowee Trace follows the Beech Grove Road for two tenths of a mile before turning off to the right. The road becomes a single track as you pass through the community of Beech Grove and then becomes gravel again at 4.7 miles. After ascending steeply, you'll pass the Beech Grove Baptist Church at 6.2 miles and, just beyond, the Waters Cemetery Road down to the left that provides access to Dick Gap Road and the Dick Gap Overlook; this is also the turnoff for the Long Trail coming from the southwest. Continue up Beech Grove Road to the Bald Knob Road at 7.2 miles and turn left. At 1.4 miles down this road, you'll see the Kentucky Trail to the left and, just beyond, parking for the Ledbetter Place Trailhead.

⑥⑧ Lee Hollow Loop ∩

5.6 miles
Moderate
Elevation change: 450 ft.
Cautions: Creek fords, steep descent
Connections: Laurel Branch Trail ∩

Attractions: This fine loop ride connects the Bear Creek Horse Camp with the Blue Heron Mining Community.

Trailhead: Follow the directions toward Blue Heron in Trail #64. On KY742, watch for the Bear Creek Scenic Area sign 3.2 miles from Revelo. Turn left. The road becomes gravel in 1.8 miles and then a one-lane road. At 2.0 miles bear right to continue toward the scenic area while the Ross Road turns left. At 2.4 miles, you'll reach a junction where you'll turn right to reach the Bear Creek Horse Camp at 3.1 miles. Drive to the back of the camp, where you'll find the trailhead. At this writing the camp is not yet open; if that's still the case when you get there, you may need to park outside the camp and ride in.

Description: Head into the woods on an old roadbed at the back of the camp. You'll pass around a gate. At 0.2 mile, you'll reach a junction with the loop. Keep straight to ride the loop clockwise. The trail leads out along a ridge above the Big South Fork.

At 0.7 mile, you'll pass a side road that drops off to the left. This is likely the route for the proposed Big Shoals Trail, which will descend the slope to the river and lead south along the river past Big Shoals. Continue straight from this junction.

You'll soon bear right and begin a descent off the ridge. At 1.4 miles the descent is steep. The old roadway had been newly graveled when we were last there, and we slid on the loose rock in the steep descent; you may want to get off and walk this descent if the surface is still loose. While descending, notice the interesting rock bluff to the right.

The trail levels off with the cove of Blair Creek to the right. But then, you'll begin another descent. At 1.8 miles, the trail switchbacks right to a level above the river where you'll now head upstream along the Big South Fork. At 2.0 miles, the trail curves right up a cove in large hemlock and hardwoods to then make a steep descent to ford Blair Creek, brown with mine drainage. From the creek, you'll make a long ascent to then continue north with the river.

At 2.5 miles, you'll curve right up the cove of Laurel Branch and begin a descent toward the creek. You'll pass a rock monolith on the left with "Laurel Branch, September 28, 1944" in fading paint on its side. Just beyond, you'll reach a junction with the Laurel Branch Trail at 2.7 miles. The trail left fords Laurel Branch and leads along an old tramroad to the Blue Heron Mining Community. Keep straight.

You'll begin a long ascent, crossing a few small streams as you climb the slope. At 3.0 miles, you'll pass an overgrown roadway to the left. At 3.5 miles, the trail passes a post and at 3.7 miles reaches a gate at the park boundary. The Lee Hollow Loop continues on the road to the right. The road beyond the gate leads out to the Mine 18 Road in another 0.3 mile; where this road emerges on the highway is 4.2 miles up from Blue Heron and 0.8 mile west of the turnoff for the Bear Creek Scenic Area.

At the gate at the park boundary, turn right to stay on the Lee Hollow Loop. You'll cross some small drainages along the way. At 4.2 miles, notice the rock shelter up to the left. A steep downhill leads to a ford of the upper end of Blair Creek at 4.5 miles. Up from the stream, you'll ride through a rock passageway and along a rock wall. Down to the right, you'll cross another branch of Blair Creek and then make a long uphill climb, passing an overhang at a reprieve in the middle of the climb. Over the ridge and down into Lee Hollow, you'll then make another long uphill climb and pass along the plateautop to close the loop at 5.4 miles. Turn left to get back to the horse camp at 5.6 miles.

⑥⑨ Split Bow Arch Loop 🚶🚶

0.7 mile
Easy
Elevation change: 100 ft.
Cautions: Rock steps, boulder passageway, wooden stairs
Connections: Bear Creek Overlook 🚶🚶

Attractions: This loop takes you through a slender arch in one of the most picturesque settings in the park.

Trailhead: Follow the directions into the Bear Creek Scenic Area in Trail #68. At the junction with the horse camp to the right, turn left. In 1.0 mile you'll reach an overlook for the arch to the right. At 1.1 miles you'll reach trailhead parking on the right. At 0.3 mile beyond this parking, you'll also find parking that will become the Bear Creek Equestrian Trailhead and, just beyond, the Bear Creek Gaging Station Road that leads a half mile down to the river to connect with the proposed Big Shoals and Huling Branch Trails. The main road continues out to US27 as KY1470 at 7.0 miles from the Bear Creek Scenic Area; this provides a shorter route if you are coming from the south.

Description: From the scenic area parking, you can walk the short trail straight ahead to the Bear Creek Overlook. But turn to the right to find the Split Bow Arch Loop leading into the woods. The trail winds down steps carved into the bedrock and reaches a junction at 0.1 mile with the loop part of the trail. Bear right to hike counterclockwise. The trail ascends to a rock wall and into a narrow passageway at 0.2 mile. You'll then come to Split Bow Arch, created by a hole in the rock wall on your left. The trail passes through the large, delicate arch by descending a wooden stairway at 0.3 mile. Turn right to continue the loop around to your left. The trail descends steps to cross a stream on a plank walkway and then ascends steps through a hemlock and hardwood forest to complete the loop at 0.6 mile. At the junction, turn right to return to the parking area.

Split Bow Arch
198

70 Yamacraw Bridge to Negro Creek 👣👣

3.0 miles one-way
(Princess Falls 1.3 miles one-way)
Moderate
Elevation change: 60 ft.
Cautions: Mudholes, creek crossings
Connections: Yamacraw Loop 👣👣, Lick Creek Trail 👣👣,
Negro Creek Trail 👣👣, Sheltowee Trace 👣👣

Attractions: This pleasant walk along the east side of the Big South Fork leads past a side trail to Princess Falls.

Trailhead: Follow the directions in Trail #64 to Stearns and stay on KY92 headed west from the junction with KY1651. You'll eventually descend into the Big South Fork Gorge, enter the NRRA, and reach the Yamacraw Bridge over the river at 6.5 miles from US27. Just before the bridge, turn right into the Yamacraw Day Use Area. Park at the trail sign. There's extra parking to the left under the bridge. The name "Yamacraw" comes Indians that lived in the region that were thought to be part of the Yamacraw tribe of South Carolina.

Description: The Sheltowee Trace National Recreation Trail passes through here. If you were hiking south on the Trace, you'd cross the river on the bridge and then turn south along the west bank of the river. For this hike, you'll follow the Trace north along the east side of the river. The trail enters the woods to the right. At 0.1 mile, the trail crosses a small streambed on a stone footbridge and reaches a junction with the Yamacraw Loop turning off to the left; this 0.4-mile loop drops down to the river and circles back to the parking area. Continue straight passing through a mixed hardwood forest with occasional hemlocks and large beech trees.

The trail drops to join an old road along the river at 0.4 mile. You'll encounter long mudholes as the trail follows the road for

199

most of the way. At 0.8 mile the trail drops to a stream crossing with a small waterfall up to the right. At 1.0 mile, a stream passes between boulders before washing across the trail. As you ascend from the small creek, you'll see Lick Creek to your left as it meanders to join the Big South Fork. You'll pass over a rise that has a good campsite and descend to an area cut with roads. Bear to the right and follow the creek upstream.

At 1.2 miles, you'll come to a junction. The main trail turns down to the left to a bridge crossing of Lick Creek. An old road leads to the right uphill. The trail in the middle is the Lick Creek Trail; a 0.1-mile walk up this trail gets you to Princess Falls where the creek spills over a shelf into a deep pool.

Continuing on the Sheltowee Trace, turn down to cross Lick Creek on the sturdy footbridge and turn left downstream. At 1.3 miles, the trail curves right to once more follow the Big South Fork downstream. At 1.5 miles the road turns down to the river, but the trail stays straight. At 1.6 miles the trail curves right up a small stream to cross it on stepping stones.

At 1.8 miles, you'll drop into a drainage region and stay along the floodplain of the river, occasionally dropping into low areas and passing stands of cane. At 2.5 miles the trail drops to a drainage branch and crosses on stepping stones.

The trail veers away from the river to the right to go up Negro Creek at 2.7 miles. Watch for a switchback left that leads down to the creek crossing at 2.8 miles; the path straight leads to an alternative crossing. Taking the first crossing, you'll drop onto boulders in the creek and then climb over a large boulder that divides the waters and then jump across to another boulder; the jump here is not recommended. Try the alternative crossing where you'll ford the creek; but if the creek is in flood stage, you may not have any choice; be careful if you jump. If you're only out for a day hike, this may be a good place to turn around.

You'll switchback up from the crossing and bear left to rejoin the river headed downstream. The trail reaches a junction at 3.0 miles below a leaning rock with the Negro Creek Trail coming in from the right. The Sheltowee Trace continues straight to Alum Ford in 2.8 miles (see Trail #75).

71 K&T Bridge 👥

0.6 miles one-way
Moderate
Mostly level
Cautions: Stream crossing
Connections: Sheltowee Trace 👥

Attractions: South from Yamacraw Bridge, you can take a short walk on the Sheltowee Trace to the K&T Bridge

Trailhead: Follow the directions in Trail #70 past the Yamacraw Day Use Area and continue across the bridge. The Sheltowee Trace crosses the Big South Fork on this Yamacraw Bridge to the west side of the river. A proposal calls for extending the trail south on the east side of the river and to make the crossing on the old K&T Railroad Bridge. For now, on the other side of the Yamacraw Bridge turn left on KY1363 and then take an immediate left on the dirt road that leads down under the bridge to the river access where you can park and walk back up the road. The Sheltowee Trace leads off the road to the south where the gravel access road makes a sharp turn.

Description: The trail heads into the woods to parallel KY1363. Bear left down stone steps to the river bank. Take care if the water is up. At 0.2 mile you'll dip through a drainage where water flows from a passageway under the highway. The trail crosses another drainage with a large culvert and then bears right up to the trace of an old road that comes down from the highway. Turn left back toward the river and continue upstream.

At 0.6 mile you'll reach the old K&T Railroad Bridge that spans the Big South Fork. The Stearns Coal and Lumber Company operated the Kentucky and Tennessee Railroad to haul coal and lumber from its camps along Rock Creek back across the river and up to the central operations in Stearns. When the bridge was built in 1907, it was the largest concrete railroad bridge in the South—575 feet long with five arches.

K & T Bridge
202

72 Koger Arch Trail 🚶🚶

0.5 mile one-way
(Koger Arch 0.3 mile one-way)
Easy
Elevation gain: 220 ft.
Cautions: Creek crossing
Connections: Sheltowee Trace 🚶🚶

Attractions: This short walk leads to an impressive arch in the Daniel Boone National Forest.

Trailhead: On the west side of Yamacraw Bridge, turn left onto KY1363. At 0.7 mile watch for the old K&T Railroad Bridge on your left. At 2.3 miles, turn left onto the graveled Beech Grove Road and cross a bridge over Rock Creek. The road becomes paved again. Watch for the trail on the left at 3.1 miles; there's room for one vehicle to park. Another half mile up the road is where the Sheltowee Trace emerges at the junction with Wilson Ridge Road.

Description: Steps take you down to cross a shallow branch of Koger Fork. You'll bear left up a ravine, but then the trail makes a sharp left and ascends, paralleling the road below on your left.

As you round the corner of a rock wall on your right at 0.3 mile, the arch appears. The mass of suspended stone, a clearance of 18 feet and a span of 91 feet, was apparently once a rock shelter, but the back part has caved in to separate the arch from the slope.

To join the Sheltowee Trace, continue on the trail through the arch and up the steps. You'll switchback several times to gain the top of the bluff and then emerge onto a dirt road at 0.5 mile. A few paces to the right, you'll connect with the Sheltowee Trace. To head north on the Trace toward Rock Creek, turn left off the road to descend through the woods. To head south and emerge on Beech Grove Road, follow the dirt road straight for a mile.

73 Lick Creek Trail 👫

4.3 miles one-way
(Lick Creek Falls 2.8 miles one-way)
(Princess Falls 4.2 miles one-way)
Moderate
Elevation loss: 460 ft.
Cautions: Creek fords
Connections: Sheltowee Trace 👫

Attractions: You'll pass two of the best waterfalls in the area plus a wet-weather waterfall in a deep rock alcove.

Trailhead: On US27 north of Stearns, on the southern end of Whitley City, turn west on KY478. In 0.3 mile you'll hit KY1651; turn left. At 1.2 miles turn right on Forest Development Road 622 and in a few hundred feet you'll see the trailhead at a gated dirt road on the left. You can also reach this point by driving KY1651 north from Stearns 1.6 miles to a left turn on FDR622. At the trailhead, there's room for a couple of vehicles to park without blocking the road.

Description: Walk up the road, following the white diamond blazes, and you'll soon cross the boundary into the Daniel Boone National Forest. At 0.2 mile the road passes under a powerline. As you continue, you'll see traces of old roads left and right, but stay with the main road straight.

At 0.8 mile the road curves left, and soon after, the trail turns right on a side road, which heads out along a ridge. At 1.0 mile the side road becomes a footpath, and at 1.1 miles you'll begin a descent into Lick Creek Gorge. Stone steps, several switchbacks, and two metal stairways assist in the descent below the rock bluff. You'll pass an overhang on the right and a tall rock bluff to pass under another overhang and at 1.3 miles turn right into a deep rock alcove encircling massive boulders that have fallen from the rock wall. A wet-weather waterfall spills from overhead as you follow the alcove around, passing under suspended rock.

204

You'll then continue your descent into coves of hemlock and rhododendron to cross a small tributary at 1.6 miles and soon after reach Lick Creek on your right; the trail now follows the creek downstream, often in the floodplain. You'll cross a couple of tributary drainages and then parallel a long, low overhang on your left and reach a junction at 2.2 miles with the trail up to Lick Creek Falls to your left; the Lick Creek Trail, continuing straight, fords Lick Creek. Turn left to get to the waterfall.

As you ascend up the side trail, you'll cross a cascading tributary of Lick Creek and continue up to a junction at 2.5 miles. The path to the right is another way back down to the Lick Creek Trail; stay straight to get to the waterfall. As you continue ascending, you'll parallel a tributary branch of Lick Creek below to your right, which is the stream the waterfall is on. At 2.6 miles, the trail bears right to cross a small stream. Then at 2.7 miles, you'll reach a tall rock wall on the left and pass into a massive rock alcove and overhang. Lick Creek Falls pours over a notch in the center of the alcove and drops 60 feet to the rocks and a pool below.

Walk back along the path from the waterfall to the fork, where you can stay left to rejoin the main trail a little farther down from where you left it. You'll descend to ford Lick Creek and rejoin the main trail at 3.2 miles; turn left.

At 3.6 miles, you'll ford Lick Creek again. During high water these fords will be impassable. At 4.0 miles, the trail runs through rocks along the creek. Soon after you'll diagonally cross an old road leading down to the creek and then rockhop a tributary stream. You'll skirt the creek once again and reach a point above Princess Falls on Lick Creek at 4.2 miles. Here the water spills over a long rock shelf that cuts diagonally across the creek. The waterfall is named for Princess Cornblossom, the daughter of Chief Doublehead. The Cherokees did not use such honorifics as "Princess," so the title was likely attached to her name by the white settlers of the region. Beyond the waterfall, a side path right drops to the pool below the falls. Continuing on the trail, you'll enter the BSFNRRA and connect with the Sheltowee Trace at 4.3 miles.

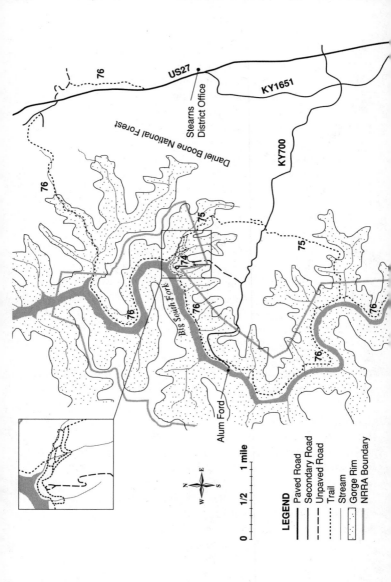

Map 13. Yahoo Falls
206

74 Yahoo Falls Trails 🏃

Topside Loop 0.8 mile
Cascade Loop 0.2 mile
Cliffside Loop 1.1 miles
Moderate
Elevation change: 250 ft.
Cautions: High cliffs, steep stairs, stream crossings
Connections: Yahoo Arch Trail 🏃, Sheltowee Trace 🏃

Attractions: You'll walk under a massive rock shelter with a slender waterfall dropping off the edge 113 feet, the tallest waterfall in the BSFNRRA and the tallest in Kentucky.

Trailhead: Just north of Whitley City on US27, turn west on KY700. Travel on KY700 through Marshes Siding as you cross KY1651; you'll soon enter the BSFNRRA and then at 4.0 miles turn right on a gravel road. If you were to keep going straight, you'd arrive at the Alum Ford River Access on the Big South Fork River. After making the turn, it's 1.5 miles down to the Yahoo Falls Scenic Area. At the one-way loop, stay to the right and drive to the backside of a picnic area to the trailhead on the right.

Description: To get to Yahoo Falls, enter the woods to walk the Topside Loop. The trail is blazed with a yellow arrow, but you'll also see a green arrow because this is also the return route for the Cliffside Loop. You'll soon see a side trail on the left that leads 50 yards down to an overlook of the confluence of Yahoo Creek with the Big South Fork. The river at this location is also the upper reaches of Lake Cumberland, created by Wolf Creek Dam far downstream on the Cumberland River.

At 0.1 mile the Cliffside Trail comes in on the left. Stay straight. You'll walk along an old roadbed until at 0.2 mile the trail bears down to the left. The trail soon switchbacks left below a couple of primitive restrooms and then right to a side path to the left that leads to an overlook of Yahoo Falls.

The main trail soon passes the top of the falls on the left and moves upstream along this tributary of Yahoo Creek. At 0.3 mile, you'll turn left to make a shallow ford of the creek and walk up to an overlook on the other side of the waterfall. The trail takes you by one more overlook before reaching a junction at 0.4 mile with the Yahoo Arch Trail, which leads 0.8 mile to Yahoo Arch.

The Topside Loop turns downhill to the left and descends through switchbacks to a junction below a rock wall with the Cascade Loop. This 0.2-mile side loop, blazed blue, passes by the Roaring Rocks Cataract where Yahoo Creek shifts through boulders as it drops steeply downstream; you'll cross the creek several times and enter the creek to pass through two boulders and reach a junction with the Cliffside Loop. Turning left up the Cliffside Loop, you'd then turn left up a connector that returns you to the Topside Loop. From the first junction with the Cascade Loop, you'll follow the rock wall along the Topside Loop to reach this other junction at 0.5 mile.

Continue from this junction, and the trail leads under the massive overhang that supports Yahoo Falls. The trail circles behind the falls while staying under the overhang to the other side. There you'll find steps that lead down to the small plunge pool. In the freezing cold of winter, a mound of radiant blue-green ice forms beneath the falls.

Continuing on the trail you'll reach a side trail to the right at 0.6 mile where the Cliffside Loop joins the Topside Loop. A little farther, another short side trail leads right to connect with the Cliffside Loop. You'll then come to a metal structure of platforms and stairs that ascends up the laurel-covered rock bluff to close the loop at 0.7 mile. Turn right to return to the parking area at 0.8 mile.

From this same trailhead, you can walk the Cliffside Loop. Instead of entering the woods to the right, walk down the road for about 50 yards and watch where the trail turns down steps to the right. The way is blazed with a green arrow. You'll see another overlook of the river. The trail bears left to circle the picnic area. At 0.2 mile the trail curves right where a path leads left up to the road. The trail then crosses a small stream on a stone footbridge. At 0.3 mile, you'll descend stone stairs to a long flight of steep metal stairs that takes you below a rock cliff. The trail then leads through several switchbacks as it descends to a junction with the Sheltowee Trace at 0.4 mile.

The Cliffside Loop now follows the Sheltowee Trace to the north. You'll first cross a bridge over the same small stream you crossed above and later turn up Yahoo Creek and pass a short connector to the Topside Loop at 0.7 mile. You'll then cross a bridge over Yahoo Creek and reach a junction at 0.8 mile where the Sheltowee Trace turns left to continue its northern traverse. The Cliffside Loop turns right.

You'll cross Yahoo Creek again, this time on stepping stones near the junction of the Yahoo Falls tributary with Yahoo Creek. The trail now passes between the two creeks. You'll soon reach a junction where the Cascade Loop comes in from the left to join the Cliffside Loop. At 0.9 mile, you'll reach a second junction where a connector turns left to ascend to a junction with the Topside Loop. Turn right. The trail leads across a bridge below the waterfall and then joins the Topside Loop. Turn right, passing the other end of the connector you passed earlier, and climb the metal and stone stairs back to the top of the cliff. Then turn right to return to the trailhead and parking area at 1.1 miles.

75 Yahoo Arch/Negro Creek/ Sheltowee Trace Loop 🚶🚶

9.9 miles
(Yahoo Arch 1.2 miles one-way)
Moderate
Elevation change: 550 ft.
Cautions: Mudholes, overgrown sections, steep descent
Connections: Cliffside & Topside Loops 🚶🚶,
Markers Arch Trail 🚶🚶

Attractions: This hike takes you to Yahoo Arch and then loops around to join the Sheltowee Trace along the Big South Fork.

Trailhead: Follow the directions in Trail #74 to the Yahoo Falls Trailhead.

209

Directions: Follow the Topside Loop for 0.4 mile past the junction with the Cliffside Loop to the junction with the Yahoo Arch Trail and turn right. At 0.6 mile, you'll cross a small side creek on stepping stones and ascend stone stairs, following Yahoo Creek upstream. Along the way, you'll cross the unmarked boundary of the BSFNRRA and enter the Daniel Boone National Forest following a white diamond blaze. From here until you reenter the BSFNRRA, the trail is open to mountain bikes.

The trail crosses another small side stream at 0.8 mile and ascends the ridge with several switchbacks. You'll reach a tall rock wall before coming at 1.1 miles to a rock overhang dripping ribbons of water at your feet. At the far end stands Yahoo Arch, an impressive span of 80 feet with an opening 10 feet high. Stone steps take you to the arch.

The trail does not pass through the arch but turns left to circle the north end. Switchbacks take you above the arch and then along a rock wall to a right turn up stone steps at 1.3 miles. You'll make a couple more switchbacks and then a gentle ascent through a drier mixed pine and hardwood forest to a junction with an old roadbed at 1.4 miles. Turn left. At 2.2 miles you'll reach KY700; just before the highway, you'll pass a half-mile side trail left that leads to Markers Arch, a 60-foot span.

When you hit the highway, turn right a few paces up the road and then turn left on graveled FDR6003. You can walk down this road to pick up the trail later on, but the trail actually turns right off the road in just 20 yards and swings around to rejoin the gravel road at 2.5 miles. From there, walk down the road to where the powerline cuts across and turn right.

The trail now drops down stairs carved into the rock. At 2.7 miles, stone steps help you over a small creek; bear left downstream. At 3.3 miles, the trail ascends over a grassy knoll where you'll find good camping. The trail gradually curves right where the creek you have been paralleling joins Negro Creek in the valley below. The trail now follows Negro Creek downstream, although so high up the slope you can't see the stream.

The trail becomes rocky. Steps are cut in a dead tree across the trail at 3.8 miles. You'll soon begin moving downhill, in some places quite steeply. At 4.5 miles the trail hits a faint roadway. Turn left a few paces and then turn right off the road. The trail drops steeply to a stream crossing at 4.6 miles and turns left down this tributary. Along the way, you'll reenter the BSFNRRA at an unmarked boundary.

The trail crosses an old road at 4.7 miles and then curves left to drop down to the old road at a "Y"; turn right on the road but then stay left at the "Y." The trail crosses another old road and then is back to a footpath. You'll descend to a junction at 5.2 miles with the Sheltowee Trace. To the left, the Trace leads toward the Yamacraw Bridge. Turn right to complete this loop hike while following the Big South Fork downstream.

The trail passes among huge boulders and then crosses a small stream at 5.3 miles; you'll see a short waterfall to the right. The trail then curves right to cross over Cotton Patch Creek where large boulders form a bridge.

Back at the river, the trail then descends the slope to cross a wet-weather stream and then a footbridge over a drainage. At 6.1 miles, you'll reach a side trail on the left to the Cotton Patch Shelter. The shelter is in disrepair, but if you want to spend the night here, you'll need to haul water from Cotton Patch Creek. Back on the main trail, you'll soon pass an old stone chimney that marks a former housesite.

At 7.4 miles you'll turn up to cross another drainage on stepping stones and at 8.0 miles reach the Alum Ford River Access that has camping and picnicking. Walk down the gravel road to a junction with KY700 at 8.2 miles with a boat ramp to the left. The trail crosses the road on a diagonal; you'll have to walk up the road several yards to where the trail reenters the woods.

The trail descends from the road and stays level. At 8.4 miles, you'll cross a rutted road. Stay to the right at a fork. The trail crosses three streams spilling over ledges and cascades. Passing below a tall rock bluff, the trail reaches a junction with the Cliffside Loop at 9.5 miles. Turn right; several switchbacks take you up the bluff to stone and metal stairs that get you on top. You'll return to the parking area and trailhead at 9.9 miles.

7️⃣6️⃣ Sheltowee Trace 🚶🏕

46.8 miles one-way
Moderate
Elevation change: 700 ft.
Cautions: Creek fords, mudholes, steep ascents and descents
Connections: Yahoo Falls Trails 🚶, Negro Creek Trail 🚶, Lick
Creek Trail 🚶, Kentucky Trail 🚶, Mark Branch Trail 🚶,
Gobblers Arch Trail 🚶, John Muir Trail 🚶,
Rock Creek Loop 🚶, Rock Creek Trail 🚶

Attractions: This long backpacking trail is also open to horses and mountain bikes in the Daniel Boone National Forest portions of the trail, but be aware you'll encounter stairs and other obstacles.

Trailhead: The 257-mile Sheltowee Trace National Recreation Trail travels north to south through the Daniel Boone National Forest in Kentucky. Toward its end, the Trace passes through the northern part of the BSFNRRA and then generally parallels the northeastern boundary to reenter the park at the Tennessee state line and end at Pickett State Park. The easiest access for the trail section that enters the BSF is on US27 2.7 miles north from KY700 in Whitley City; you'll pass the Stearns District Office of the national forest along the way. The Trace can also be accessed at Yahoo Falls, Alum Ford, Yamacraw Bridge, and Peters Mountain Trailhead and in the national forest at the Hemlock Grove picnic area and Great Meadows Campground on FDR137.

Description: While traveling through the remote woods of Kentucky in February 1778, Daniel Boone was captured by a band of Shawnees, who took him to one of their towns along the Ohio River. Boone escaped four months later, but during his stay, Chief Black Fish grew to like him and gave Boone the name Sheltowee, meaning "Big Turtle." The Sheltowee Trace, named in Boone's honor, has an occasional blaze in the shape of a turtle, but most frequently, a white diamond blaze.

From the trailhead on US27, you can turn right to hike the

Trace northeast 20.4 miles to Cumberland Falls State Park. But to head toward the Big South Fork, go straight, away from the highway, to pass under a powerline and enter the woods and bear left. You'll emerge onto a gravel road at 0.7 mile. Turn left. You'll pass some houses and at 1.0 mile reach a church and a sawmill on US27. Cross the highway onto a paved road that curves right over railroad tracks. At 1.3 miles, at a side road to the left, the trail ascends into the woods on the left. At 1.4 miles, the trail dips to join an old road bearing left. You'll cross under a powerline and join another dirt road.

At 1.6 miles, the trail turns left off the road onto a path. You'll descend into a hollow and reach a gravel road at 1.9 miles. A few paces to the right the trail reenters the woods. You'll pass under a powerline, and reach a switchback right down through rocks at 2.2 miles to enter Big Creek Gorge. The trail swings through a rock shelter with the North Fork of Big Creek streaming off the lip in wet weather at 2.3 miles. The trail circles along the rock bluff and then descends to cross a small stream at 2.4 miles at a low overhang. Descend to rockhop the North Fork at 2.5 miles. The trail now follows the creek downstream, crossing it nine times before emerging onto a gravel road at 3.2 miles. Turn right on the road and then left back into the woods.

At 3.4 miles, you'll climb up a bank to an old road. Turn left to a hunting cabin on a private inholding within the national forest; do not trespass. The road makes a sharp curve left here, but the trail stays straight onto a side road in front of the cabin. Stay with this side road and watch for a turn left off the road and descend stone steps to a ford of Big Creek at 3.6 miles.

You'll ascend from the creek and cross the boundary of the national forest into the BSFNRRA. As you near the confluence with the Big South Fork, the lower part of Big Creek is flooded with the waters of Lake Cumberland. At 3.9 miles, the trail curves left as it turns upstream along the Big South Fork.

At 5.8 miles, massive rock walls stand to your left as you enter the Yahoo Falls area. You'll then follow Yahoo Creek upstream. The trail crosses a tiered boardwalk over a drainage. You'll reach a junction at 6.2 miles with the Cliffside Loop to the left that leads up to Yahoo Falls. Bear right to cross Yahoo Creek on a bridge and ascend stone steps and reach another junction at 6.3 miles; a connector trail to the left leads to the Topside Loop. The Trace continues down Yahoo Creek to soon curve left and once more parallel the Big South Fork upstream.

After crossing a bridge over a tumbling stream, you'll reach another junction with the Cliffside Loop at 6.6 miles. From here the Sheltowee Trace continues south along the Big South Fork. At 8.1 miles you'll cross KY700 at the Alum Ford River Access and reach the junction with the Negro Creek Trail at 10.9 miles (see Trail #75 for details). At 11.1 miles, you'll ford Negro Creek and at 12.7 miles cross Lick Creek on a bridge and reach a junction with the Lick Creek Trail to the left. You'll arrive at Yamacraw Bridge on KY92 at 13.9 miles (see Trail #70).

Walk up to the highway and cross the bridge over the river. Turn left on KY1363; then turn off the paved road on the gravel road that leads down to the river access; in just a few yards, the trail leads off into the woods. You'll then parallel KY1363 along the river to the old K&T Railroad Bridge at 14.5 miles.

Just past the bridge, you'll reach the confluence of Rock Creek with the river. The trail follows Rock Creek upstream. You'll pass traces of coal mining—cables and slag piles and, if you can see through the trees to the right, a large concrete support structure. At a junction at 14.8 miles you'll turn left to descend to a ford of Rock Creek; watch for deep mud along the bank. If the water is up, do not ford; instead take the alternate route to the right at the junction. You'll walk up to the old railbed of the K&T and turn right to walk past the old support structure and out to KY1363. Then walk left on the paved road to a left turn on Beech Grove/Devils Creek Road to either take the Koger Arch Trail to reconnect with the Trace (Trail #72) or continue to where the Trace joins the road in 2.6 miles from the junction at the Rock Creek ford.

If you can make the ford at Rock Creek, you'll have left the BSFNRRA and reentered Daniel Boone National Forest. On the other side, you'll follow an old railbed along Grassy Fork Creek. The trail reaches a junction at 14.9 miles with the northern end of the Kentucky Trail to the left. Stay straight.

At 15.1 miles you'll pass some old foundations remaining from the coal mining days; the mines opened on the slopes above and the coal was hauled out on the narrow-gauge train that ran along the railbed you're walking. At 15.3 miles, ford Grassy Fork at the site of a bridge where the rail line once crossed the creek; you'll see rockwork that supported the span. At 15.4 miles, ford the creek above a small cascade. You'll enter an open area at 15.5 miles. Back into the woods, you'll pass through a rock passageway that the train must have barely cleared and ford the creek four times.

You'll cross a tributary of Grassy Fork and then reach a fork in the roadway; stay right. The path crosses the tributary again and ascends to turn right and pass under a powerline at 16.4 miles. Ascending on an old road, you'll pass back under the powerline and ascend to a junction with another road; turn right.

As you ascend, watch for where the road splits at 16.7 miles; there you'll bear right on a path that's easy to miss. Following the path to the right, you'll ascend to a junction with a road at 16.9 miles. Across the road and to the right is the end of the Koger Arch Trail. The Sheltowee Trace turns left to follow the road out to the Beech Grove Road at 17.9 miles at the junction with the Wilson Ridge Road.

Now walk up the paved road. At 18.1 miles, watch for where the Trace leaves the road to the right on a dirt road that ascends into the woods. A bar across the road prevents vehicle access. The trail ascends steeply to the top of the ridge. Continue along the ridgeline with views of the Rock Creek and BSF Gorges.

At 19.0 miles you'll descend exposed sandstone and then remain along the ridgeline until at 19.4 miles the trail descends stone steps through a rock gap. The trail curves left around a point of the ridge and ascends back to the ridgetop.

You'll connect with an old road; bear right. At 20.4 miles, the trail turns right off the road in a descent. The trail connects with a road at 21.0 miles; turn right. At 21.1 miles, make a sharp left on another road. At 21.3 miles cross a small stream on stepping stones and pass a housesite marked by yucca plants. Soon after, you'll rockhop a wider stream in a beautiful hemlock cove. Trace Branch flows on your right. At 21.4 miles the trail fords the branch but in a short distance fords back; if the water is too high, just bushwhack upstream; be careful on the steep slope. Continue up the old roadway to another ford of Trace Branch at 21.6 miles.

On the other side, head up the slope in a steep ascent to turn left on an old roadway at 21.9 miles. You'll soon turn right off the road. On top of a ridge, follow a road through a logged area with a stand of young pine to reenter the woods and turn right off the road at 22.7 miles.

Ascending a bluff, you'll enter a forest of tall pines to connect with an old road at 22.9 miles; turn left. At 23.2 miles a road comes in from the right; stay straight. When the road forks, stay to the right up to the graveled Laurel Ridge Road at 23.3 miles; turn right. At 24.4 miles, the road becomes dirt and soon passes a fenced cabin. This marks the end of the improved road, and from here on you'll encounter mudholes and a rough road that's nearly impassable to four-wheel drive vehicles.

At 24.7 miles, where a side road goes straight, the road curves right into a steep descent to a shallow crossing of a fork of Puncheoncamp Branch at 24.9 miles. You'll then have a steep ascent to get back up to the top of the plateau.

The road reaches a junction at 26.2 miles where Laurel Ridge Road turns to the left. The road to the right leading past a cabin is FDR6301. After making the left turn, you'll pass a cemetery where some of the Blevinses and Kidds are buried. The road then curves right at 26.3 miles where a side road leads past a clearing to the left. This old road will eventually be the Cat Ridge Trail that leads down toward the river.

At 26.7 miles, the road forks, but you can go either way because the two forks soon come back together. Then at 27.5 miles, you'll reach a junction with a road to the left that is the route for the Kentucky Trail and the Difficulty Creek Trail. Continue straight. You'll have a steep ascent and then level off in a more open area where the road is muddy in wet weather.

You'll reach a junction with the graveled FDR6101 at 29.0 miles. Turn left to reach a junction of roads at 29.2 miles. Up to your left, you'll find the Peters Mountain Trailhead. Straight ahead is FDR569, also called the "Peters Mountain Road." To the right is FDR139 that leads toward the Bell Farm Horse Camp. The Sheltowee Trace heads to the right on a path into the woods.

Soon the trail descends into a cove and crisscrosses Mark Branch at 29.8 miles. Rockhop a side stream and cross Mark Branch again to reach the top of Mark Branch Falls. The trail swings right and switchbacks left in a descent into the plunge basin. At 30.3 miles you'll pass behind the 50-foot waterfall.

The trail soon crosses the creek below the waterfall and continues down the cove. From here on, the trail fords Mark Branch 11 times. At 31.4 miles, you'll reach a junction with the Mark Branch Trail to the left that leads up toward Peters Mountain Road. Continue straight and you'll cross Mark Branch four more times. The trail emerges into an open area at a junction at 31.8 miles. The Trace turns left here, but you can also follow a side path straight ahead to a ford of Rock Creek in 0.1 mile to get to the Hemlock Grove Picnic Area on FDR137. A bridge is scheduled to be constructed soon.

Turning left, you'll reach a junction at 31.9 miles with the Gobblers Arch Trail that takes off to the left to form a loop with the Mark Branch Trail. Continue straight. You'll parallel Rock Creek upstream and at 33.9 miles pass a path down to the right to a ford across to the Great Meadows Campground. At 36.4 miles, you'll reach a junction with a path to the right that fords Rock Creek to FDR137; just to the right up that road is the end of the Parkers Mountain Trail. Continue straight.

The Trace crosses a boardwalk over Massey Branch at 36.5 miles. You'll ascend to cross a small drainage on a footbridge and reach a junction at 36.8 miles with the John Muir Trail. Continue straight. The JMT and the Sheltowee Trace now coincide; this is also the Rock Creek Loop (see Trail #44).

At 40.2 miles, you'll reach a junction with the Rock Creek Loop turning up left and the JMT/Sheltowee Trace turning right to ford Rock Creek. On the other side, turn left upstream to cross into Pickett State Forest. A concrete piling perched on a rock on the other side of the creek once supported a railroad bridge.

You'll then connect with the Rock Creek Trail at 40.4 miles. You have the option of continuing straight on the Rock Creek Trail, passing the junction with the Tunnel Trail and fording the creek three times to reach TN154 at 40.3 miles (Trail #84). Another option is to turn left on the Rock Creek Trail; you'll ford the creek to the other side and then make a steep ascent to connect with the Hidden Passage Trail at 41.9 miles. Turn left and continue on to emerge at the trailhead for the Hidden Passage Trail on TN154 at 46.8 miles (Trail #83).

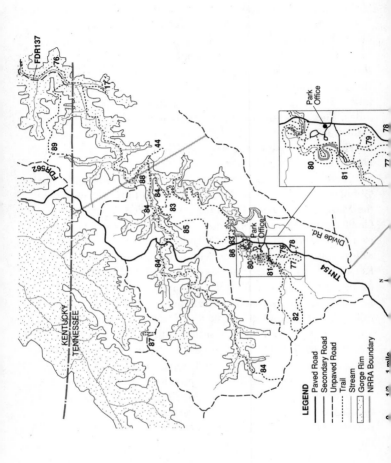

Map 14. Pickett State Park and Forest
218

77 Hazard Cave Trail Loop 🚶🚶

2.5 miles
(Hazard Cave 0.2 mile one-way)
Moderate
Elevation change: 200 ft.
Cautions: Steep concrete stairs, creek crossings
Connections: Indian Rockhouse Trail 🚶🚶, Ridge Trail Loop 🚶🚶,
Lake View Trail 🚶🚶, Natural Bridge Trail Loop 🚶🚶

Attractions: Tennessee's Pickett State Park and Forest, with arches and rock shelters, lies adjacent to the Middle Creek area. With the same geology and similar topography to the BSFNRRA, the state park should be included in your visit to the area.

Trailhead: North on TN154 from Divide Road, you'll pass through Pickett State Forest and at 0.8 mile enter Pickett State Rustic Park. In another 0.2 mile, the trailhead for Hazard Cave lies on the left. The Indian Rockhouse Trail begins across the road.

Description: You'll descend gravel-filled steps and concrete steps to access the Hazard Cave Loop, which has a white blaze. Turn left to reach Hazard Cave. You'll descend another long flight of concrete steps and curve left to a footbridge across a drainage at the base of a long rock wall. The trail then follows the wall to Hazard Cave, a large rock shelter with a sand floor at 0.2 mile.

At the far end, the trail ascends from the opening and swings left to another exposed part of the bluff. The trail curves right and drops to a crossing of a small creek at 0.5 mile. You'll then have a long downhill to another creek crossing. At 0.9 mile, the trail drops into a cove where you'll cross a creek at a small waterfall; you must step down the two-foot ledge. Drop steeply to cross the creek again. At 1.2 miles, you'll reach a junction with the green-blazed Ridge Trail Loop. Turn right.

Soon after, you'll reach a junction where the Ridge Trail turns left across a bridge over Thompson Creek. Turn right. This

Hazard Cave

220

section is also blazed green because this is the access to the Ridge Trail from the picnic area; it's also part of the Lake View Trail, blazed grey. At 1.4 miles, you'll reach another junction. A path straight ahead leads into the picnic area, and there a side path, blazed white, leads right to the Recreation Lodge. Turn right at this junction; this route also has a brown blaze because this is a connector to the Natural Bridge Trail Loop.

The trail now ascends. At 1.6 miles you'll pass two paths left to the Natural Bridge Trail. At 1.9 miles, you'll pass a third connector to the Natural Bridge Trail. Stay straight. The trail soon tops the ridge. At 2.4 miles, a path left leads up to the trailhead. The trail straight ahead is the completion of the loop to your beginning point below the first set of stairs. Turn left to get back to the parking area.

78 Indian Rockhouse Trail 𝍖

0.2 mile one-way
Easy
Elevation loss: 100 ft.
Connections: Hazard Cave Trail 𝍖

Attractions: The trail ends at a sweeping rock overhang that may be largest in the Big South Fork region.

Trailhead: Follow the directions in Trail #77 to the Hazard Cave Trail parking area.

Description: On the other side of the highway the Indian Rockhouse Trail drops gradually 0.1 mile to an overlook where you'll see the rock shelter below and to the right. Continue from here as the trail descends and then circles right into the rock shelter. Although the trail ends, you can enjoy a walk through the massive 250-degree circular structure. A small pool at the center is fed by water falling 60 feet from the rim above.

7⑨ Natural Bridge Trail Loop 👣👣

0.7 mile
Easy
Elevation change: 100 ft.
Cautions: Steep stairway
Connections: Hazard Cave Trail Loop 👣👣

Attractions: You'll pass two natural arches—one large, one small—on this stroll through the woods.

Trailhead: Follow the directions in Trail #77 into Pickett State Park and pass the Hazard Cave Trailhead. In another 0.3 mile into the park, you'll find parking for the Natural Bridge on the left.

Description: From the parking area, you'll step down to a junction, which is the loop trail left and right. Turn right to get to the Natural Bridge. The trail curves down stone steps to the top of the arch. A side trail to the right leads across the top of the arch and heads into the woods to connect with the road into the picnic area in half a mile.

Turn left to descend steep rock steps and then curve right to get to the bottom of the arch, sometimes called "Highway 154 Natural Bridge." This is an exceptionally thin arch, with a span of 86 feet and a clearance of 23 feet.

Walk under the arch to where the trail heads straight out through a forest of hardwood and laurel. The trail is blazed brown. At 0.1 mile, you'll cross a footbridge over a wet-weather drainage and continue down and turn left to again cross the drainage on a footbridge at 0.2 mile. The trail ascends up the hollow and switchbacks right up a slope to reach a junction at 0.3 mile. Straight ahead, the trail leads 0.2 mile to another junction where the left fork connects to the Hazard Cave Loop in 0.2 mile and the right fork heads down to the picnic area.

To complete the Natural Bridge Loop, turn left at the first junction. Continue an ascent of the slope until at 0.4 mile, you'll reach another connector that leads right 0.1 mile up to the Hazard Cave Loop. Continue straight. The trail curves left at a rock wall where you'll find another natural arch. The smaller opening penetrates the ridge. The trail then curves right around the point of the ridge and swings left at the head of a deep hollow.

At 0.6 mile the trail narrows with a rock wall on the right and a dropoff into the hollow on the left. You'll then skirt the highway and walk along the top of a bluff to complete the loop at 0.7 mile above the Natural Bridge. Turn right up to the parking area.

⑧⓪ Lake Trail/ Island Trail Loops 👭

3.0 miles
Easy
Elevation change: 100 ft.
Cautions: Swinging bridge
Connections: Lake View Trail 👭, Bluff Trail 👭,
Ladder Trail 👭

Attractions: You'll hike around the park lake to pass by an arch that spans lake waters.

Trailhead: At 1.0 mile into Pickett State Park on TN154, you'll see the office/visitor center and two roads to the left. Take the first road into the picnic area. Begin your walk at the swinging bridge that crosses Pickett Lake.

Description: Cross the bridge to a shelter overlooking Pickett Lake. To the left lies the Lake View Trail to the south. Turn right; the Lake Trail with a red blaze climbs some rock stairs and then follows the bluff above the lake's swimming and boating area.

At 0.2 mile, the trail turns left with a side path continuing straight to a grudging overlook of the Pickett Lake Natural Bridge; you'll get better views later. After turning left, you'll encounter a junction with a side trail to the left that connects with the Lake View Trail behind the shelter above the swinging bridge. Stay straight ahead to keep on the main trail. In 0.7 mile, you'll find

223

a rest shelter to the right.

At 1.0 mile a short side trail leads down to the Thompson Creek Dam that backs up Pickett Lake. The Civilian Conservation Corps built the dam in the 1930s. From the top of the dam, you'll get the best view of Pickett Lake Natural Bridge stretching across an arm of the lake. The bridge is an incised meander where Thompson Creek folded back on itself to eventually punch a hole through the ridge to make the bridge. The bridge was eventually left high and dry as the creek continued to erode, cutting its valley deeper. At one time a narrow-gauge railway, used to haul lumber out of the area, paralleled Thompson Creek and passed under the natural bridge. The construction of the Thompson Creek Dam brought the water back to a level with the bridge opening. Today you can rent boats and float under the bridge.

Continue on the Lake Trail. At 1.5 miles, the Bluff Trail leads left to TN154. Bear right, passing down to a footbridge over Thompson Creek below the dam. A slight climb from the creek takes you through hemlock and rhododendron to a junction with the Ladder Trail, which also leads out to TN154. You'll pass a side path to another rest shelter.

At 2.0 miles, the Island Trail leads to the right over the top of Pickett Lake Natural Bridge where you can see the Thompson Creek Dam below. The half-mile Island Trail loops around the peninsula, past another rest shelter, and returns over the natural bridge to this junction at 2.5 miles. To the left, a short path leads up to the campground at site #29.

Continuing on the Lake Trail, you'll pass behind the park chalets and drop to cross a small wet-weather stream and then ascend past another shelter at 2.8 miles. Afterwards, follow the blazes up to the left through the cabins to emerge onto the cabin road. Turn right along a fence to a gap where the trail turns down stone steps and crosses a gravel service road behind the boating area. You'll then bear left upstream along a small creek to a right turn over a footbridge. The trail leads on to the Recreation Lodge and the picnic area at 3.0 miles where you began the hike.

⑻⒈ Lake View Trail 👣

0.7 mile one-way
Easy
Elevation change: 50 ft.
Cautions: Steep stairs
Connections: Lake Trail 👣, Ridge Trail 👣,
Hazard Cave Loop 👣

Attractions: You'll have views of Pickett Lake from atop a bluff at the water's edge.

Trailhead: Follow the directions in Trail #80 into the picnic area and cross the swinging bridge over the lake.

Description: On the other side of the bridge, ascend steps to get above the shelter and turn left to hike the Lake View Trail. The Lake Trail leads to the right.

Heading south on the Lake View Trail, you'll walk along a bluff above the lake across from the picnic area. With Thompson Creek backed up by the dam to create the lake, you'll see deep emerald-green pools. The trail bears right through the forest to cross a stream at 0.3 mile on a footbridge. You'll then turn downstream, passing a small waterfall in the creek. The trail reaches the lake again and continues upstream.

At 0.4 mile, you'll swing right around a shelter where you can rest on a bench. At 0.5 mile you'll reach a junction with the Ridge Trail to the right. Stay straight to cross Thompson Creek on a bridge and reach a junction with the Ridge Trail and Hazard Cave Loop to the right. Turn left and stay straight past a connector to the Natural Bride Trail to get back to the picnic area at 0.7 mile.

82 Ridge Trail Loop 🕺

3.0 miles
(Under-Bluff/Over-Bluff Loop 1.8 miles)
Moderate
Elevation change: 150 ft.
Cautions: Creek ford
Connections: Hazard Cave Trail Loop 🕺, Natural Bridge
Trail Loop 🕺, Lake View Trail 🕺

Attractions: This is a pleasant walk with rock shelters and rock bluffs.

Trailhead: Follow the directions in Trail #80 to the Pickett State Park picnic area. At the far end of the picnic area, 0.5 mile from the turnoff on TN154, you'll find the trailhead.

Description: This trailhead is an access point for several trails in the park, so you'll see white, gray, brown, and green blazes. For the Ridge Trail, you'll follow the green blaze.

Head straight into the woods. Almost immediately, you'll encounter a trail to the left that leads to the Recreation Lodge that you passed on the road into the picnic area. Stay straight.

You'll soon come to a trail to the left that is part of both the Natural Bridge and the Hazard Cave Loop Trails. Again stay straight. The trail descends gradually to cross a small stream on a footbridge and reach a junction with the loop part of the Ridge Trail. To the right a bridge crosses Thompson Creek and also gives access to the Lake View Trail. Keep left to hike the Ridge Trail clockwise. You'll ascend to another junction where the Hazard Cave Loop comes in from the left. Stay right, and you'll cross the park boundary into the contiguous Pickett State Forest.

From this junction, you'll descend to an inclined bridge that spans Thompson Creek where Natural Bridge Creek joins it on your right at 0.3 mile. The trail then passes through the bottom-land of rhododendron, laurel, and small hemlocks between the two creeks. You'll ascend into a drier forest of laurel and pine, cross a region of thin soil and exposed rock with reindeer moss, and follow a ridge up to a junction at 0.6 mile. From here you can keep to the left to hike over the bluff or right to walk under the bluff; walking under the bluff is more interesting, so stay to the right.

The trail drops below the bluff line where you'll pass several overhangs in a rock wall on your left; at 0.7 mile the trail passes under a small rock shelter. Finally, you'll ascend to a junction with the over-bluff route at 0.9 mile. If you are out for a shorter hike, you can use this under-bluff/over-bluff loop to return to the trailhead for a walk of 1.8 miles.

Continue straight in a hardwood forest atop the ridge. You'll ascend to pass through an understory of young pine at 1.2 miles. The trail curves right to encounter a rock bluff. Bear left to pass along the bluff and then turn right to climb to the top. You'll see an old road to the left, but stay right to walk along the edge of the bluff. At 1.4 miles the trail begins a descent from the bluff and then curves right to head back toward the park. The trail bottoms out in a hollow and sinkhole area at 1.7 miles. You'll then ascend slightly into a more moist area and reach a ford of Natural Bridge Creek at 1.8 miles. If the water is up, you'll have to wade.

From the ford, the trail follows a small tributary upstream. The trail curves right and left to reach the bluff above Natural Bridge Creek. The trail curves left to pass through a couple of hollows and once more reaches the bluff above the creek; you'll see bare rock at the bluff edge on your right at 2.4 miles.

The trail swings through another hollow and crosses the boundary from the state forest back into the state park and drops to a junction with the Lake View Trail at 2.8 miles. Turn right to complete the loop. You'll cross the bridge over Thompson Creek and close the loop at 2.9 miles. Turn left to walk back to the trailhead at 3.0 miles.

83 Hidden Passage Trail Loop 👫

10.0 miles
Moderate
Elevation change: 100 ft.
Cautions: High bluffs, stream crossings
Connections: Rock Creek Trail 👫, Sheltowee Trace 👫,
John Muir Trail 👫, Tunnel Trail 👫

Attractions: Small arches, waterfalls, numerous rock shelters, and the Hidden Passage make this one of the most interesting trails in Pickett State Park and Forest.

Trailhead: Head north from the park office on TN154. In 0.3 mile you'll see the Hidden Passage Trailhead on the right. There's room for only two vehicles to park.

Description: As you walk into the woods to begin the Hidden Passage Trail, you'll find the way marked with green blazes and occasionally the shape of a white turtle. The turtle signifies this is also part of the Sheltowee Trace National Recreation Trail, which travels south from Kentucky through the northwest portion of the BSFNRRA to end at Pickett State Park. This part of the Hidden Passage Trail is also one alternative for the ending of the John Muir Trail, which travels north from Leatherwood Ford in the BSFNRRA and then swings west to also end at Pickett State Park.

The trail passes through woods of pine, mixed hardwood, and laurel. In spring you'll notice birdfoot violets, yellow stargrass, and bluets. Climbing fern decorate the shrubs as Thompson Creek flows downstream on your right, creating a gorge that will grow deeper as you continue on the trail.

You'll follow a side creek upstream and cross at a spillway. The hollow of the stream contains hemlock and rhododendron. This stretch of trail is typical of the Hidden Passage Trail, meandering across the top of the plateau in predominantly pine and mixed hardwoods and periodically dropping into coves where the hemlock and rhododendron predominate.

At 0.5 mile, you'll reach the junction with the loop part of the trail, you can walk left or right, but the best approach is to walk right, hiking counterclockwise. You'll soon encounter a small arch created by a short column of rock supporting an overhang. Turn right and descend to a large overhang where the passageway through rocks is somewhat "hidden."

At 0.7 mile, a short side trail takes you down to the foot of Crystal Falls. This tributary spills down two steps into a green pool of water before making its way toward Thompson Creek.

Back on the main trail, you'll climb up stone steps and then cross the stream just above Crystal Falls. Watch your step. The trail parallels the gorge for a time and then turns away from the rim. You'll find the loop periodically swerves from the edge of the gorge but then later returns.

At 1.3 miles, the trail reaches a bare rock overlook of the gorge and then turns away from the gorge edge. You'll cross a jeep road at 1.5 miles. Then at 1.8 miles the trail swings right while a side trail to the left leads to a low rock shelter. From here the trail passes many rock shelters and overhangs, some quite large and long. Many of these have benches inside, built by the Civilian Conservation Corps in the 1930s when the park was being developed out of Stearns Coal and Lumber Company land donated to create the park and forest.

At 2.1 miles you'll dip into a long rock hollow sheltered by thick rhododendron and with a wet-weather waterfall in the center. When you emerge, watch for a huge hemlock balanced at an angle on your left. At 2.4 miles the trail passes under a powerline.

At 2.8 miles you'll reach a narrow section of the trail with a rock bluff on your left and Thompson Creek Gorge on your right. Around a point, you'll find a long rock overhang and then a long rock wall. At 3.2 miles, the trail crosses a stream on a stone walkway. Then at 4.0 miles you'll come to a large rock shelter that sweeps around in a 180-degree curve; a small waterfall spills from the lip of rock overhead. After another rock overhang, you'll reach at 4.2 miles the 1-mile side trail to Double Falls, which is on a tributary of Thompson Creek. This side trail, marked with a white blaze, drops from the bluff to Thompson Creek at 0.7 mile. Keep following the trail and you'll reach a

229

fork where you can turn down to the creek across from the confluence of a tributary. To get to Double Falls, stay left. The trail descends to the creek, which you must wade across unless the weather has been dry enough you can rockhop. The trail then curves right to follow the tributary upstream to a rock alcove that contains the picturesque two-step waterfall, each drop about 10 feet.

From the junction with the side trail to Double Falls, you'll switchback up and walk along the bluff to Thompson Overlook at 4.4 miles, where you'll have views of the gorge. You'll find here the end of a road that has come from the Group Camp in the park; vehicles are not allowed past the Group Camp. You can shorten your walk by taking this road left. You may camp at the overlook.

At 5.0 miles, you'll cross a stream on a bridge and come to a junction with the Rock Creek Trail marked by a brown blaze. Both the Sheltowee Trace and the John Muir Trail leave the Hidden Passage Trail at this point, following the Rock Creek Trail to the right.

After this junction, the trail switchbacks up, crosses a jeep road, and switchbacks down into a hollow to a junction with the one-mile Tunnel Trail marked with a blue blaze at 5.4 miles. This side trail leads to an abandoned railroad tunnel and to a junction with the Rock Creek Trail.

From the Tunnel Trail junction, you'll switchback up and walk along the bluff of the gorge of Rock Creek. The trail bears away from the gorge, crosses a jeep road, and passes under a powerline at 6.2 miles. At 7.5 miles, you'll emerge onto the road running from the Group Camp to Thompson Overlook to the left. Turn right and walk down the dirt road to the Group Camp; bear left around the compound until at 8.5 miles the trail turns left off the road to reenter the woods. You'll walk along the top of a circular rock wall and at the far end pass over a small arch.

The trail descends to a rock shelter and at 9.1 miles crosses a stream at the top of a small falls. The trail ascends and crosses an old road and drops to the junction at 9.5 miles where you first encountered the loop. It's then a half mile back to the trailhead.

84 Rock Creek Trail 🏃

8.4 miles one-way
Moderate
Elevation change: 250 ft.
Cautions: Dropoffs, steep downhill, numerous creek fords
Connections: Hidden Passage Trail 🏃, Rock Creek Loop 🏃,
Tunnel Trail 🏃, John Muir Trail 🏃, Sheltowee Trace 🏃

Attractions: This trail follows Rock Creek and forms a loop hike with the Hidden Passage and Tunnel Trails.

Trailhead: Follow the directions in Trail #83 along the Hidden Passage Trail to the junction at 5.0 miles with the Rock Creek Trail. You can also reach this point by hiking out the road behind the park's Group Camp 1.2 miles to the Thompson Overlook and picking up the Hidden Passage Trail there; north along the trail from the overlook, it's 0.5 mile to the beginning of the Rock Creek Trail. If you want to walk the Rock Creek Trail from the other direction, drive north from the turnoff to the park's Group Camp 1.3 miles to where TN154 crosses Rock Creek and turn right just before the bridge, down beside the creek; follow the road to the right, watching for a left turn off the road in 0.1 mile as the trail fords Rock Creek. You can also access the trail from the west end on Boundary Road, a gravel road marked by a stone pillar off TN154 south of the park entrance and south of Divide Road; at 3.7 miles along this road that follows the boundary of Pickett State Forest, you'll find the trailhead on the right.

Description: Turn east off the Hidden Passage Trail half a mile north of Thompson Overlook on the Rock Creek Trail, which has a brown blaze. Both the John Muir Trail and the Sheltowee Trace coincide with the Rock Creek Trail.

The trail skirts the northern edge of a hollow containing a small creek. You'll hear a waterfall in the grotto below, unless it is the dry season. At 0.5 mile you'll reach the gorge of Thompson Creek and curve left to follow the bluff high above the creek with steep dropoffs to the right. Along the way, a few stone steps take

231

you to a higher level.

At 0.8 mile, the trail joins a faint road and turns right to follow the old roadbed down a ridge into the gorge. The trail turns left off the roadbed at 1.1 miles in a steep descent to a more level area above the creek and then another steep descent to Thompson Creek; the descent includes a step down a rock shelf that's slippery in wet weather. The trail then leads left down Thompson Creek in hemlock and rhododendron. At 1.4 miles, Thompson Creek flows into Rock Creek.

The trail now turns upstream along Rock Creek to a ford at 1.5 miles. On the other side you'll find a junction with the John Muir Trail/Sheltowee Trace to the right. Turn left to complete the Rock Creek Trail, headed upstream. This part of the Rock Creek Trail is an alternative for completing the John Muir and Sheltowee Trace Trails into the state park. The trail follows an old lumbering railbed remaining from when the Stearns Coal and Lumber Company operated in the region. At times, the trail goes along the creek edge. At 1.8 miles the trail is almost in the creek, and it may be covered in high water, in which case you must find a place to climb around or wade in the creek.

You'll pass along a rock bluff to a junction with the Tunnel Trail at 2.5 miles. The Rock Creek Trail turns right at this junction while the Tunnel Trail heads steeply down to a creek ford and then up the other bank to an abandoned railroad tunnel carved into the rock ridge. The Tunnel Trail, which does not pass through the tunnel but turns right to pass up and over the tunnel, can be used to loop back to the Hidden Passage Trail. This makes a good five-mile loop hike.

You may reconnect with the Rock Creek Trail through the tunnel, or from the junction with the Tunnel Trail, continue on the Rock Creek Trail by turning right along a rock wall with the creek below on the left. You'll drop steeply into a ravine with a small waterfall in an alcove to the right. At 2.6 miles the trail drops steeply again to ford a small tributary of Rock Creek, and later another tributary stream runs under the trail in a culvert. At 2.7 miles, you'll arrive at a junction with the path through the tunnel; here a bridge carries you over Rock Creek to the mouth of the tunnel.

Stay right at the junction to continue on the trail, now following the old railbed again. You'll ford Rock Creek at 2.8 miles. At 3.0 miles you'll step over a trickle of water that runs across the trail; it forms a small waterfall up to your left. You'll ford the creek again at 3.2 miles and walk up a washed out area where the trail turns left. The trail then curves right to stay on the old railbed; you'll pass a road to the right and then reach another ford of Rock Creek at 3.3 miles.

The trail leads up to a gravel road; turn right on the road to a road junction that leads left up to TN154 at 3.4 miles. Here is the secondary access for the trail; you may camp in this area. On TN154 turn north to walk across the bridge over Rock Creek and then turn left off the road back into the woods, now following a double blaze of blue and white.

At 3.5 miles, you'll ford Rock Creek, the first of 29 crossings in the next four miles of this section of trail, along with several crossings of small side streams. At low water, you'll be able to rockhop most crossings; at times of high water, the trail is impassable, and so you should not attempt this section.

This Rock Creek Trail/John Muir Trail alternative continues to follow the old railbed along Rock Creek; you'll often walk along an artificial ridge on which the narrow-gauge railroad ran, and you'll occasionally see depressions in the ground left from the decomposed ties.

After #11 crossing at 5.2 miles, you'll come to some metal pieces left from the railroad operation. At #18 crossing at 6.1 miles, you'll see a rail lying beside the trail. After #22 crossing at 6.8 miles, notice the creek flows under massive boulders that create a passageway. You'll make #25 crossing at 7.3 miles on a swinging bridge. At #28 crossing at 7.6 miles, you'll see the remains of a wooden bridge just downstream; there would have been bridges at all the crossings when the railroad was operating. You'll make #29 crossing at 7.7 miles on a wooden bridge. Afterward, the trail turns up left to leave Rock Creek. You'll ascend through a drier forest and emerge on Boundary Road at 8.4 miles.

85 Tunnel Trail 👣👣

1.0 mile one-way
Moderate
Elevation loss: 225 ft.
Cautions: Creek ford
Connections: Hidden Passage Trail 👣👣, Rock Creek Trail 👣👣

Attractions: This short connecting trail passes by a couple of small arches and takes you to an old railroad tunnel.

Trailhead: Follow the directions in Trail #83 along the Hidden Passage Trail to the junction with the Tunnel Trail 1.0 mile west of Thompson Overlook.

Description: The Tunnel Trail, with a blue blaze, descends north from the Hidden Passage Trail. The trail curves left in its descent to pass over a ridge and then switchback right. The trail then curves left, eventually passing around the point of a ridge to arrive at a rock wall and a wooden bench at 0.1 mile. Facing the rock wall, you'll see a small arch up to the left.

The trail then follows the rock wall, gradually descending and passing a small rock shelter. At 0.2 mile, you'll arrive at a rock overhang with another bench. A small arch there has four openings. The trail begins descending again at 0.3 mile.

Toward the end of your descent, you'll pass over the old railroad tunnel and circle right and down to stand in front of the tunnel at 0.9 mile. The tunnel, which has been carved through the rock, gives access to the Rock Creek Trail on the other side of the ridge. The Tunnel Trail turns left away from the tunnel and drops steeply to a ford of Rock Creek and then ascends the opposite bank to a junction with the Rock Creek Trail at 1.0 mile. The Tunnel, Rock Creek, and Hidden Passage Trails form a nice loop hike.

🕯🕯 Ladder Trail/ Bluff Trail Loop 🏃

1.8 miles
Moderate
Elevation change: 130 ft.
Cautions: Ladders, creek ford
Connections: Hidden Passage Trail 🏃, Lake Trail 🏃

Attractions: You'll see interesting rock overhangs and ledges along Thompson Creek.

Trailhead: Follow the directions in Trail #83 to the Hidden Passage Trailhead.

Description: From the parking area, walk south down the road and cross Thompson Creek on the highway bridge. At 0.1 mile, turn right on the Ladder Trail. Just up the road, you'll see another access to the Ladder Trail, but take this first trail.

Follow the brown blaze of the Ladder Trail on a bluff above Thompson Creek. A rock wall lines the trail on the left. At 0.2 mile, the trail drops below a tall rock bluff to emerge on a shelf over the creek. You'll climb down a green metal ladder to get to creek level; the stream flows under the ladder. At the bottom, continue for several yards to a ford back across the creek. You'll then climb a wooden ladder to get back on the rock shelf.

The trail then continues along the rock wall, passing a wooden bench below an overhang and then another. You'll pass beyond the rock wall for a walk in the woods to a four-way junction at 0.6 mile. The trail to the left is the connector that leads out to TN154 just up the road from where you began the Ladder Trail. The middle trail leads 0.1 mile up to the campground at site #13. To continue on the loop hike, take the right trail that leads down to a junction with the Lake Trail at 0.7 mile. Then turn right to drop across a bridge over Thompson Creek.

At 0.8 mile, you'll reach the junction with the Bluff Trail. Turn right. The yellow-blazed Bluff Trail follows the bluff above

Thompson Creek downstream. You'll cross footbridges over side streams, pass rock overhangs, rest on benches along the way. At 1.3 miles, the trail crosses a small footbridge that spans water running off the rock wall. You'll then turn steeply up to the left. The trail soon forks; stay to the right. The left fork is an old route that is now abandoned; above, you'll see where it comes back in to the present trail. Then the trail stays fairly level through the woods to emerge on TN154 at 1.8 miles. You'll see to the right just down the road the Hidden Passage Trailhead where the loop hike began.

87 Kentucky View Loop 👣

0.2 mile
Easy
Elevation change: 60 ft.
Cautions: Dropoffs
Connections: None

Attractions: This short walk offers a grand view north into Kentucky.

Trailhead: North from the park headquarters along TN154, turn left at 3.5 miles on the graveled Kentucky Cut-Off Road. Watch for parking and the trailhead on the right in another 2.0 miles.

Description: Walk up the trail into the woods. In 100 yards, you'll reach a junction that is the loop part of the trail. Turn right to walk the loop counterclockwise.

The trail skirts the edge of a bluff to reach the point of the ridge and the view north at 0.1 mile. You'll have a sweeping view down Flint Fork Cove north into Kentucky.

Continue on the loop to circle back to the junction; watch for massive rock walls in the cove to your right. Then retrace your steps back to the trailhead.

88 Coffee Trail 👥

0.5 mile one-way
Moderate
Elevation loss: 300 ft.
Cautions: Steep descent, creek ford
Connections: Rock Creek Loop 👥, Sheltowee Trace 👥,
John Muir Trail 👥

Attractions: This trail provides short access to the Rock Creek Loop in the BSFNRRA.

Trailhead: At 4.6 miles north of the visitor center on TN154, turn right on Coffee Road, a dirt road that is passable to passenger cars in dry weather. If the road is muddy, you'll need to park wherever you can and walk the road 1.2 miles to Coffee Overlook. The trees have grown up at the overlook so that you do not have much of a view, but you can see the bluffs above Rock Creek through the trees. The trail begins to the right, blazed orange.

Description: The trail descends from the road to a house-sized boulder sitting on the point of the ridge. You'll turn right here to descend steeply and curve left toward Rock Creek. At 0.3 mile, the trail levels off on a bench and then descends again to the floodplain of the creek where you'll turn right to cross a small side creek above its confluence with Rock Creek. You'll soon cross the boundary into the BSFNRRA. The trail follows a ridge along Rock Creek, part of the old Stearns lumbering rail line that once operated in this gorge.

The trail soon turns left off the old railbed to a ford of Rock Creek and, on the other side, a junction with the Rock Creek Loop. This is also the Sheltowee Trace and the John Muir Trail; all three trails coincide here.

⑧⑨ Buffalo Arch/Parkers Mountain Trails 🚶🚶

2.0 miles one-way
(Buffalo Arch 0.4 mile one-way)
Moderate
Elevation loss: 100 ft.
Cautions: May be closed for deteriorating stairs
Connections: Sheltowee Trace 🚶🚶

Attractions: A side trail leads to the unique Buffalo Arch while the main trail connects with Rock Creek and the Sheltowee Trace.

Trailhead: From the Pickett State Park office, drive north on TN154 5.1 miles to the Kentucky State line. In another 0.3 mile, turn right on the graveled Forest Development Road 562 and enter the Daniel Boone National Forest, which abuts the BSFNRRA on the north. In another 0.8 mile, turn right on FDR6305, a dirt road that's not marked. Because of the roughness of the road from here on, you may not want to proceed without four-wheel drive, although it should be passable in dry weather; if you park here, do not block the road. Walk down the dirt road, which makes a sharp curve downhill to the right. Stay with the dirt road until at 0.3 mile you'll reach the trailhead on the left. At this writing, the Parkers Mountain Trail is closed due to a set of stairs that needs replacing, which should take place sometime soon.

Description: Before walking the Parkers Mountain Trail, keep straight on the road to Buffalo Arch. An overgrown side road leads to the left; keep straight. At 0.3 mile, you'll reach a turnaround in the road, although the road keeps going. The Buffalo Arch Trail heads into the woods on the right. The trail descends left into a cove, crosses a small creek over a metal culvert, and ends under the arch at 0.4 mile. The huge arch, with a clearance of 19 feet and a span of 82 feet, is at the end of a ridge. The ridgeline descends across the back of the arch into the small valley

Buffalo Arch

created by the Right Fork of Pennington Branch. So the arch looks like a flying buttress holding up the hillside.

Retrace your steps back to the beginning of the Parkers Mountain Trail and head up the path. At 0.2 mile, the trail parallels an old logged area to the left, and you'll soon cross a road. Soon after, the trail crosses the trace of another road. At 0.8 mile, you'll skirt the logging road to cross a side road and stay on the path into the woods; watch for the white diamond blazes to stay on the trail. Soon after, the trail veers to the left.

You'll begin a gradual descent at 1.3 miles. The trail swings right to a switchback left and then reaches a set of metal stairs at 1.5 miles that descends a low bluff. At this writing, the stairs are deteriorating and the trail has been closed for safety; hopefully the stairs will have been repaired and the trail reopened when you hike this way.

The stairs descend into the head of a hollow where a small wet-weather waterfall spills down the rock wall. At the bottom of the stairs, turn right. The trail then curves left to a flight of stone steps that drop among large boulders and rock walls to curve right again.

At 1.6 miles, you'll swing under a low overhang on the left. The trail crosses a small stream emerging from rocks and then another emerging from under a huge boulder. You'll circle right to cross the second drainage again and descend to a gravel road at 2.0 miles. This is FDR137 that parallels Rock Creek below. You can walk to the left to reach the Great Meadows Campground in 2.8 miles. Or you can walk to the right for 0.1 mile to where the road swings down to a ford of Rock Creek and connects with the Sheltowee Trace on the other side.

The Forest Service plans a new Rock Creek Trailhead at this end of FDR137 for access to the Sheltowee Trace and the Parkers Mountain Trail. To drive to here, you can continue north on FDR562 from the turnoff for the Parkers Mountain Trail for 7 miles to the beginning of FDR137. Or if you are coming from the north on KY1363 from the Yamacraw Bridge, when the pavement ends, bear right on the graveled FDR564 to the junction of FDR562 and 137. Then head down FDR137 for 7 miles past the Hemlock Grove Picnic Area and the Great Meadows Campground to the junction with the Parkers Mountain Trail.

Selected References

Des Jean, Tom. Unpublished paper. "Prehistory—Introduction and Conceptual Framework," National Park Service, BSFNRRA.

Howell, Benita J. 1981. *A Survey of Folklife Along the Big South Fork of the Cumberland River*. Knoxville: The University of Tennessee.

Humphrey, Steve E. 1981. "The History of the No Business and Station Camp Communities," unpublished manuscript, National Park Service, BSFNRRA.

Manning, Russ. 1994. *Exploring the Big South Fork, A Handbook to the National River and Recreation Area*. Norris: Mountain Laurel Place.

—————. 1993. *The Historic Cumberland Plateau, An Explorer's Guide*. Knoxville: The University of Tennessee Press.

National Park Service. 1995. *Roads and Trails Management Plan Draft*. BSFNRRA.

Stanley, Steven M. 1986. *Earth and Life Through Time*. New York: W. H. Freeman and Co.

Thomas, J. Patrick. 1989. *Lore & Legend, History Magazine*, Vol. 1 No. 1. Devoted to the history of the Stearns Coal & Lumber Company.

U.S. Army Corps of Engineers. 1976. *Big South Fork General Design Memorandum* and *Final Environmental Impact Statement*. Nashville.

Trail Index

Hiking 🚶🚶

242

243

Addresses & Phone Numbers

Bandy Creek Stables
P.O. Box 191
Huntsville, TN 37756
615/879-4013

Big South Fork Motor Lodge
P.O. Box 252
Stearns, KY 42647
606/376-3156

Big South Fork National River and
Recreation Area
Rt. 3 Box 401
Oneida, TN 37841
615/879-3625 or 879-4890 (Bandy
Creek Visitor Center)
423/569-9778 (Park Headquarters)
606/376-3787 (Blue Heron Mining
Community)
606/376-5073 (Stearns information
center)

Big South Fork Scenic Railway
P. O. Box 368
Stearns, KY 42647
606/376-5330 or 1-800-462-5664

BSF Station Camp Wilderness Resort
Rt. 2 Box 169-A
Oneida, TN 37841
423/569-9847

Bruno Gernt House
Estate of Bruno Gernt
Box 69
Allardt, TN 38504
1-800/771-8940

Charit Creek Lodge
250 Apple Valley Road
Sevierville, TN 37862
423/429-5704

Clear Fork Farm Bed & Breakfast
328 Shirley Ford Road
Robbins, TN 37852-9605
423/628-2967

Daniel Boone National Forest
Stearns Ranger District
P.O. Box 429
Whitley City, KY 42653
606/376-5323

Grey Gables Bed & Breakfast
P.O. Box 5252
Rugby, TN 37733
423/628-5252

Historic Rugby, Inc.
P.O. Box 8
Rugby, TN 37733
423/628-2430

Marcum-Porter House
P.O. Box 369
Stearns, KY 42647
606/376-2242

Pickett State Rustic Park
State Hwy. 154
Jamestown, TN 38556
615/879-5821

Other Books from Mountain Laurel Place

Exploring the Big South Fork
A complete handbook to the geology, biology, and history of the Big South Fork National River and Recreation Area plus many details on outdoor activities, including hiking, horseback riding, paddling, and mountain biking. 240 pp., color and B&W photos, maps. $15.95

Tennessee's South Cumberland
(2nd Edition)
A hiker's guide to trails and attractions of Tennessee's South Cumberland Recreation Area, Fall Creek Falls and Cumberland Mountain State Parks, Franklin and Prentice Cooper State Forests, plus several natural areas and pocket wildernesses. 135 pp., photos, maps. $8.95

The Historic Cumberland Plateau
(published by the University of Tennessee Press)
An explorer's guide to the history and the outdoors of the Cumberland Plateau in Tennessee, Kentucky, and Alabama, providing historical background and giving specific directions on how to explore the region. 360 pp., photos, maps.
$14.95 paperback, $29.95 hardback

The Best of the Great Smoky Mountains
A hiker's guide to trails and attractions of the Great Smoky Mountains National Park of Tennessee and North Carolina. 256 pp., photos, maps. $10.95

Historic Knoxville and Knox County
(Bicentennial Edition)
A walking and touring guide to the historic city center, neighborhoods, parks, and back roads of this Tennessee city and county. 256 pp., photos, maps. $4.95 (Regular $8.95)

(Order Form on back)

Order Form

Send check or money order to:
Mountain Laurel Place
P.O. Box 3001
Norris, TN 37828

Telephone
423/494-8121

Title	Price	Quantity	Total
Exploring the Big South Fork	$15.95		
Tennessee's South Cumberland	$ 8.95		
The Historic Cumberland Plateau	$14.95		
hardback	$29.95		
Best of the Great Smoky Mtns.	$10.95		
Historic Knoxville & Knox Co.	$ 4.95		
Trails of the Big South Fork	$12.95		
Subtotal			
Tenn. residents add 8.25% sales tax			
Shipping and handling*			
Total enclosed			

*Add $2.00 for shipping/handling if ordering one book or for each book if separate mailing is requested. **We pay for shipping/handling if more than one book is ordered and mailed in one shipment to the same address.**

Ship to _____

Address _____

_____

Items offered subject to availability. Prices subject to change without notice.